SS

D1201362

Seventy-Five Years in Education

Seventy-Five Years in Education

The Role of the School of Education,
New York University, 1890–1965

by ELSIE A. HUG

NEW YORK UNIVERSITY PRESS   1965

Frontispiece: The Original Home of the School of Pedagogy 1890–1896.

For
Albert Barrett Meredith
Educator, Statesman, Friend

This short book by Professor Elsie A. Hug tells the story of the School of Education from its earliest beginnings and its founding in 1890 up to the present time. Ours was the first school for preparing teachers, administrators, and educational specialists to be established in a major university. We are extremely grateful to Dr. Hug for writing what is more than an excellent history of one institution. She has related with keen insight and understanding the development of education in the United States during the period from 1890 to 1965 and has pointed out the important role our School played during these years.

The School of Education has now completed seventy-five years of facing problems and difficulties, seventy-five years which have resulted in substantial achievement and progress. During this period we have often been in the forefront of educational activity and advancement. As we celebrate our Diamond Jubilee year we are grateful for the sound foundations and structure our earlier colleagues built. They have left us a glorious heritage and one of America's best professional schools. Our present faculty and those who will join us during the next few years have an unprecedented opportunity to create *the* School of

Education of the future. The history of the next twenty-five years could well tell another success story of the preparation of superior teachers and leaders, the discovery of new knowledge through research and experimentation, and enlightened educational services to mankind at home and abroad.

Walter A. Anderson

DEAN, SCHOOL OF EDUCATION

September, 1964

In the concept of history, seventy-five years is but a moment in time. In the assessment of a social institution, seventy-five years takes on significance.

The rapidity and extensiveness with which the School of Education of New York University has developed makes for a voluminous record to be critically analyzed and appraised if a thorough historical study is to emerge. Further, such a study would require detailed consideration of the cultural milieu as it impinged on education.

The time available for the task, the recency of a good part of the record, and the close identification of the writer with the institution under discussion has militated against the objectivity essential for such a thorough appraisal. In fact, without the guidance and assistance of officers of administration of the School of Education and some members of the faculty, the project would not have progressed this far.

Through the committees of the School of Education, practically every full-time member of the faculty renders service to the institution and, implicitly thereby, to the profession. This fact, together with the breadth of outside interests and activities of the group, made it difficult to refrain from naming the entire faculty. Some criteria had to be invoked, and three were applied in reaching decisions regarding individual identification. Such identification was made in the case of persons who:

1] were or are members of the administration of the School,

2] were identified with pioneering or unique efforts in the teacher education division, and

3] through long association have become identified with a particular phase of the program or other aspect of the School's work.

Where the book fails to name persons who should have had such recognition, the responsibility for these omissions must be borne entirely by the author.

The present volume represents a review of the origin and development of the teacher-education unit at New York University. It remains for a future historian to produce the evaluative study which the School of Education deserves.

This manuscript had gone to press when the School of Education suffered a great loss in the untimely death of Dean Walter A. Anderson. There is every evidence that his forward-looking leadership has left an indelible mark on the progress of this institution and on American education. John C. Payne has been named Acting Dean of the School of Education.

Elsie A. Hug

NEW YORK
AUGUST, 1964

CONTENTS

Part I
How It All Began

1 · Cultural and Institutional Antecendents

The sober appearance of the Gothic edifice situated on the east side of Washington Square gave little evidence, in the year 1880, of the turmoil and activity taking place behind its gray stone walls. The structure, erected in 1835, was the second home of the University of the City of New York chartered under that name in 1831. The first official lectures had been given in Clinton Hall at the corner of Beekman and Nassau Streets.

By 1880 the University consisted of the four-year undergraduate liberal arts college known as University College, established in 1832; the Medical College, opened in 1841; a School of Civil Engineering and Architecture, introduced in 1854, later called the School of Applied Science and ultimately the College of Engineering; and the School of Law, founded in 1858. Despite the sentiments expressed by the founding fathers to establish in New York City a university dedicated to the common man and to his practical pursuits, it will be noted that, consonant with the prevailing pattern of higher education, the liberal arts college was the first division to be named.

Following establishment of the Law School, no changes were incorporated until 1886 when, in response to pressure from qualified applicants, a Graduate Division was added. Agitation for graduate instruction had been building in the nation generally, and this, together with popular demand and local pressure, had led most universities to offer advanced, postgraduate study by the 1880s. The Graduate Division in the University of the City of New York operated within the administrative structure of University College. The School of Pedagogy was established on March 3, 1890.

In 1896 the name of the institution was changed from the University of the City of New York to New York University.

The next structural modification occurred in 1903 when the Collegiate Division was set up to accommodate nongraduates, especially from the School of Pedagogy, who wished to take such work as would qualify them for a bachelor's degree. In 1913 this division became the coeducational undergraduate liberal arts college called Washington Square College.

The affairs of the University of the City of New York were administered by a chancellor, a vice-chancellor and a governing body of prominent citizens called the Council of the University. The individual colleges or schools each were headed by a dean.

The turmoil which the institution was experiencing in its fiftieth year grew out of difficulties—financial and otherwise—which had reached such a crisis that the University had been threatened with the necessity of closing its doors. Among the issues which led to this condition, were the following:

1] the absence of adequate endowment,

2] the questionable standards for admission and graduation due to the proprietary method under which these units were conducted (the faculty being wholly dependent for support upon student fees),

3] the failure on the part of the University to introduce post-graduate work, and

4] the stagnation of University College due to three main reasons:

    a] its presence in the midst of a business section and its attendant lack of college life,

    b] free tuition in University College (from 1870 to 1893),

    c] its lack of sectarian connection.

Within a quarter of a century the first of these reasons listed as a detriment was hailed by Chancellor Henry M. MacCracken as an actual asset for many thousands of students when viewed with respect to the extreme accessibility of the University. As of the year 1880, no women were admitted to the University. However, this fact is not listed as an item contributing to its difficulties.

Despite these plaguing problems the University did not close its doors. In fact, it was on the threshold of pioneering in the area of teacher training at the university level. Back of this decision lay the long story of the emergence of teaching as a profession and of the preparation of teachers as a separate academic discipline.

EARLY REFERENCES TO TEACHER TRAINING

In America, the idea that teachers should be specifically

trained for their craft appeared as early as the eighteenth century. Benjamin Franklin harbored it and, with certain reservations, recommended the practice as a suitable function of his academy at Philadelphia in 1789. But the efforts of Franklin and others in the direction of formal teacher training had no lasting effect since, before any movement forward in this direction could be achieved, education itself had to be set firmly on its feet. It took three more decades to reach this objective.

The practical realization of a free, tax–supported common school provided the first significant impetus to concern for better qualified teachers. For example, in 1823 Samuel R. Hall opened the first normal school in the United States at Concord, Vermont. In 1827 James G. Carter founded a similar institution in Lancaster, Massachusetts. Both of these were private schools.

As early as 1826, Governor Clinton, of New York, recommended to the legislature the establishment of a seminary for the education of teachers in the monitorial system of instruction. Apparently no action followed this recommendation, but in 1827 the governor recommended the creation of a central school in each county for the education of teachers. In that same year the New York legislature appropriated money to aid the academies in promoting the education of teachers—the first state aid in the United States for teacher training.

When, in 1831, a group of farsighted citizens petitioned the State of New York for incorporation of the University of the City of New York, they declared an intention to include a program for the preparation of teachers for the common schools. They went so far as to create a Chair

of Pedagogy and appointed the Rev. Thomas H. Gallaudet
to it. This gentleman had been pleading the cause of formal preparation of teachers through a series of articles in
the Hartford, Connecticut, *Observer* over a period of years
beginning in 1825. Although the stated objective of the
group petitioning for a university which would offer such
instruction preceded the great reform movement of
Horace Mann, Henry Barnard, and others and predated
by eight years the opening of the first state normal school
at Lexington, Massachusetts, in 1839, the educational
aspiration was in advance of the academic realization.
While Gallaudet would appear to have been a logical
choice for the assignment, he never filled the post and it
was left vacant for almost sixty years. Implementation of
the intention had to wait until cultural forces had made
their impact felt in the nation and particularly in the city
of New York. The nineteenth century had all but run its
course before this occurred.

SOCIAL AND EDUCATIONAL CHANGE—1880–90

During this long hiatus America successfully sur-
mounted its growing pains and gave early promise of the
leadership it was to take in world affairs. Expansion was
the keynote of the age—from natural boundaries to intellectual achievement. This was the era of the virtual
disappearance of the frontier and the appearance of technology as the driving force in American life. Agrarianism
as a chief occupation gave way to industrialism; the humanities in considerable measure gave way to science; and
a relatively ethnically cohesive population became a heterogeneous mass, spreading from coast to coast but depositing

great clusters of immigrants in the industrial zones, especially along the eastern seaboard. These conditions effected
spectacular changes in urbanization, means of production,
transportation, and communication. In back of all this
was the phenomenal growth in the population which,
swelled by the floods of immigration, saw the census
figures rise from 23,191,876 in 1850 to 63,622,250 in 1890.

These social changes were accompanied by significant
developments in the field of education. In the last decades
of the nineteenth century, pedagogical pioneers such as
Henry Barnard, William H. Payne, and Elmer Ellsworth
Brown (who later became the seventh chancellor of New
York University) were writing the first American treatises
in the history and philosophy of education. The efforts
of such men as William T. Harris, B. A. Hinsdale, Charles
DeGarmo, and G. Stanley Hall resulted in opening up
formal study in psychology; Joseph Mayer Rice, Edward
L. Thorndike, John Dewey, and others were devising
systematic investigations into the actual products of classroom teaching.

The emphases growing out of the scientific movement
in education played a large part in the introduction of
graduate study in American higher education during this
period. A basic change in the character of higher education took place, and Berelson has noted that ". . . the
graduate school was in the forefront of the movement as
supplier of teachers and the model of learning." [1]

Nowhere, perhaps, was the impact of the national
changes more strongly felt than in New York City. In fact,

[1] Bernard Berelson, *Graduate Education in the United States*,
p. 13.

as the city grew in size, complexity, and importance, it became almost a self-contained reflection of these forces which were influencing national change. If anything, because of its polygot nature, the problems the city faced were more acute.

THE CULTURAL AND EDUCATIONAL SCENE IN
NEW YORK CITY—1880–90

Population Change

By 1880 New York City was a thriving metropolis. Manhattan Island was still somewhat isolated from its sister boroughs, for the connecting bridges were still a decade away and the subways were a product of the next century.

Possibly the major characteristic of the city's cosmopolitanism was the significant transformation of its population. Blake reported over five million arrivals from foreign shores in the 1880s, with over eighty percent of them concentrated in the northeast industrial zone.[2] Of these five million, census statistics reveal, 901,643 remained in New York City. This figure represented thirty-five percent of the city's population of 2,507,414. Of the foreign-born group, 96.5 percent emigrated from northwest Europe.

Social Change

In this last decade of the nineteenth century, the city presented a façade of light and shadow. As workers crowded into the urban centers, amid desperate conditions

2 Nelson M. Blake, A Short History of American Life, p. 470.

of squalor and overcrowding, there was a mushrooming of
slum areas that constituted serious threats to civilian
health and welfare. These conditions spawned the de-
grading sweatshops and their shameful corollary—child
labor. Yet, on Fifth Avenue between Fiftieth and Eightieth
Streets was the world-famous "millionaire's row" which
consisted of block after block of imposing mansions designed by the new world's ablest architects for the new
world's new nobility. That nobility constituted the finan-
ciers and industrialists who played such prominent roles
in advancing the nation's economic power.

At the other end of the spectrum were the factory
workers, most of foreign extractions. For New York City
these represented the largest occupational group. The
greatest proportion of persons was employed in manufac-
turing and trades, while the smallest proportion was
represented in education.

By 1890 it was estimated that there were 40,000 children
of compulsory school age who were not in school at all.
Many of these children were exploited by their families
to supplement the family income, and, although the
compulsory education law required all children between
the ages of eight and twelve to attend school all of the
time the schools were in session from October through
June, children between the ages of twelve and fourteen
years were permitted to go to work provided they attended
school eighty days during the school year. Thus, the provision of this law was in conflict with the child labor law
which prohibited employment of children under fourteen
years of age.

Some idea of the ratio of teaching personnel to pupil

enrollment between 1880 and 1900 can be gained from the figures given below:

Year	Estimated Population 5-18 Years	Pupils Enrolled	Teachers Male	Female	Total Number Teachers
1880	15,379,000	10,001,000	122,500	171,300	293,800
1890	18,897,000	13,050,000	123,400	245,000	368,400
1900	21,983,000	15,689,000	126,500	305,300	431,800

Again, the tabulation represents national statistics. Comparable figures for New York City are unavailable prior to the consolidation of the boroughs into Greater New York in 1898. This is due, in part, to the fact that at the time the city was consolidated there was no uniformity in the schools of the different boroughs, either in organization or operation.

The Status of Education in New York City

The economic want of the tenement house neighborhoods compelled large numbers of boys and girls to leave school to begin earning as soon as the compulsory law allowed. Superintendent William Jansen has pointed out that the education these children received was sufficient to create in some a desire for things higher and better than those which many found in their sordid surroundings, but it was not enough to give them any practical preparation to enable them to earn a decent living. Further, of the half million pupils enrolled in elementary schools, only 13,700 were graduated, and of this number only fifty percent registered for further schooling. Out of this situation came a recommendation for the establishment of a well-equipped trade school for such pupils.

Although New York City had taken the lead in setting up the first evening school in America in 1823, it was the last large city to establish public high schools. At the time of the consolidation into the city of Greater New York, there were thirty-three evening elementary schools in Manhattan and ten in Brooklyn. The record indicates that the first evening high school in the country was started in New York City in 1866. It antedated the establishment of the day high schools by thirty years. Students who were graduated from elementary school and who wished to continue their education were accepted in the College of the City of New York or the Normal College (now Hunter College). These institutions had five-year courses, the first year of which was on a secondary school level.

The Demand for Improved Teacher Qualifications

The swelling enrollments in the elementary schools, the growth of interest in manual training classes as adjuncts to the general school program and the trade schools, together with the efforts made by in-service teachers toward self-improvement all had their impact on the status of teacher education in the years between 1880 and 1890.

While there were nine normal schools throughout New York State in 1887, there was only one such educational facility in New York City, the Normal College previously referred to, now Hunter College. One such college was entirely inadequate to supply the teachers for a continually expanding city school system. In addition, it has been conceded generally that the normal schools actually were often little more than higher elementary schools and that their chief functions were to strengthen the common branches and to offer minimum training in pedagogies.

There was indeed an urgency for some source of instruction in New York City whereby the inexperienced teacher could learn his craft and the teacher in service could improve himself through the more advanced study of educational principles, practices, and problems. The University of the City of New York accepted this challenge, and its first gesture was to restore the Chair of Pedagogy, unoccupied for more than half a century.

In 1887 Jerome Allen, formerly president of the state normal school in Minneapolis, Minnesota, was appointed to teach several courses in pedagogy. Within the year a second professor was appointed to teach additional courses and the vice-chancellor reported to the University Council:

The call upon the University to do work for teachers does not diminish. Besides the college graduates enrolled in the Graduate Division there are about 175 hearing the lectures in the week. . . . The subject of a School of Pedagogy as well as a decision whether women as well as persons of the male sex shall be admitted to the post graduate courses, is engaging the Board of Visitors and Graduate Committee who will report progress tonight. . . . Inquiry respecting our work in this branch has come to the Vice-Chancellor from many quarters, even from as far as Jena in Germany.

Interest in the new program of studies grew, and the results of the offerings were so salutary that the School of Pedagogy was established in 1890. This was the first purely professional school for teachers on the graduate level.

2 · The School of Pedagogy 1890–1920

The formal founding of the teacher-education unit of the University of the City of New York is recorded in the minutes of the University Council for March 3, 1890. The School of Pedagogy, as it was called, was the first such school to hold equal rank with other professional schools, such as law and medicine, within the structure of a university.

The minutes further reveal that, in the thinking of the University administration, women were to play an important role in the development of the institution, and particularly in the affairs of the newly created School of Pedagogy. Hence, at this meeting a second action was taken establishing the Women's Advisory Committee.

This committee was empowered to make its own bylaws, appoint its own officers, and formulate plans and make recommendations for the advancement of the University's work for women. As in the case of all University committees, such plans and recommendations were subject to the approval of the University Council. In a circular of information issued later in the same year, Vice-Chancellor Henry M. MacCracken called attention to the fact that the University of the City of New York was the first such institution to call women to assist in conducting its affairs. This was a fitting step for the University to take, he maintained, since women were entering the teaching profession in increasing numbers and the profession was exerting a greater influence than ever before.

The group of women comprising this committee did not look upon their affiliation as an empty gesture on the part of the administrative officers. They maintained a close scrutiny over the units within the institution already admitting females and worked zealously to extend their admission to other divisions within the University.

The nature and extent of the activities of this body included:

1] correspondence with other institutions with a view to securing suggestions for the work of the committee,

2] investigation of means within the University for ascertaining the needs of women students and for consideration of measures for their welfare,

3] provision of scholarships, and

4] supervision of all public meetings in which the "interests of women students are any way involved."

A report of the treasurer for 1892 notes gifts made to the endowment, library, and scholarship funds of the School of Pedagogy, adding the comment, ". . . the only department where, thus far, we have been called upon especially for financial assistance." The treasurer concluded her report with the caution: "It should be remembered . . . that this is a Committee advisory, not to the School of Pedagogy, but to the Council. This field of action is the whole University."

Despite this note of mild censure, until its dissolution in 1913 the Women's Advisory Committee continued to devote its major efforts in behalf of the School of Pedagogy. That the Women's Advisory Committee was a militant and effective guardian of the institution's welfare will become clear as the record of its activities is revealed.

AIMS AND PURPOSES

During the first half of its thirty-year tenure, the policy of the faculty of the School of Pedagogy with regard to its character and standards was indeterminate. Three factors contributed to this condition: (1) the School was the first of its kind established as part of an American university. There were, therefore, no precedents for guidance; (2) the content of pedagogy was only now beginning to be organized and adapted to the needs of American life, and (3) the student body to be served by the institution had not been clearly defined.

Despite these elements of confusion, the catalogues of the School of Pedagogy carried statements of aims and purposes which were modified three times within its thirty-year span. These statements indicated sensitivity to the contemporary concern with the science of education, in each instance emphasizing provision of instruction in psychology (descriptive, experimental, physiological); in practical administration; comparative education (comparative study of national systems of education); the principles and art of teaching; and in sociology. At the same time it was evident that the total program was to include work in the liberal arts and the humanities, as, for example, courses in history, logic, ethics, philosophy, and aesthetics.[1]

The paragraph on aims and purposes, which appeared in the catalogue for 1906–07 and which was retained until the division was completely reorganized in 1921, contains the following statement:

It (the School of Pedagogy) seeks especially to meet the needs of students of superior academic training and of teachers of experience who are prepared to study educational problems in their more scientific aspects and their broader relations.

Thus the work in pedagogy at the university level may be assumed to have been more comprehensive and of greater depth than that generally to be found in the normal schools. An intention on the part of the leadership of the School to build a quality institution also may be implied from the reference to "students of superior academic training and of teachers of experience."

In each of the three catalogues cited, attention was called to the superior advantages of New York City as a rich laboratory in which to study pedagogical problems.

ORGANIZATION AND ADMINISTRATION

At the time of its establishment the teacher-education unit was headed by a dean and three faculty members. Professor Jerome Allen, who had taught the courses in pedagogy between 1887 and 1890, filled the post of dean. After his death in 1894, Dr. Allen was succeeded by Edgar R. Shaw, who served until 1900.

The founding of a School of Pedagogy by title did not

[1] *Catalogues* of the University of the City of New York for: 1892–93, p. 86; 1896–97, p. 160; 1906–07, p. 172.

insure autonomy in the conduct of its affairs. The Chair
of Pedagogy, first referred to in 1832 and restored in 1887,
was under the jurisdiction of a body called the Graduate
Division. Originally set up with the University College to
open the way for graduate work in the University, this
body was described as follows: "This Division includes
all examinations and courses of instruction offered by the
University to candidates for the degree of M.A., M.S.,
or Ph.D." [2]

A Council action taken at the time of incorporation of
the School of Pedagogy directed that the Committee of
the Graduate Division ". . . shall supervise the School in
addition to its particular work." This arrangement continued for two years, but was superseded by a resolution
adopted by the Council on May 27, 1892, which stated
that, ". . . the whole administration of the School of
Pedagogy shall be directed by the Faculty which shall
consist of the professors of the School, with the Chancellor; the paid lecturers to be advisory members but with
no vote."

In spite of this resolution, the ten gentlemen constituting the Graduate Division continued to act in an advisory capacity. The extent of their role in decision-making
may well be pondered since the voting members of the
faculty of the School of Pedagogy (including the dean)
matched the number making up the Graduate Division in
only three of the thirty years of the School's existence.
Further, while the annual reports of the chancellor of the
University contain extracts from reports submitted by

[2] Catalogue, University of the City of New York, 1886–1887,
p. 12.

the dean of the School of Pedagogy, there are no references to the manner in which policy was established or
executed. For example, the University archives reveal no
statements relating to a rationale governing the early operation of the division nor any indication of the body in
which responsibility for the establishment of policy was
to be vested. It is only as recommendations for change in
policy are introduced that prevailing philosophy can be
adduced.

As late as 1913 the School of Pedagogy operated to a
great extent as a department in the Graduate School of
Arts and Science. The shaping of its curriculum and the
control of its policy still remained largely outside the
pedagogy faculty. There is nothing in the record to indicate any significant change between 1913 and 1920. It
would appear, therefore, that in the matter of independent
development, while the School of Pedagogy had identity
in name, it had little autonomy in function.

The confusion arising from a lack of homogeneity in the
student body, together with the limited control over policies and program, left a skeletal organism with administrative problems but too little authority to solve them. The
dean had to concern himself primarily with matters of
finance and with internal morale, and the faculty taught
their classes largely on a proprietary basis with compensa-
tions being determined by the student fees collected.

The only evidence of resistance to this situation is found
in the concerted action of the faculty in 1900 in which
criticism was made regarding policies and methods of
administration. Once again, lack of precedent was cited
as a basic cause for the condition which arose.

The Chancellor earnestly advised the faculty members to come to a harmonious agreement among themselves without making an appeal to the corporation. This counsel, however, was not accepted, and in the winter of 1900–01, the three professors formulated charges against the dean charging him with violation of the University statutes and with faculty methods which were greatly to the prejudice of the School. The dean, on his part, charged the professors with making his position intolerable by their persistent opposition and personal assaults.

A committee of the University Council, which included a sub-committee of the Women's Advisory Committee, heard both the faculty and the dean and, following its deliberations, recommended that the chairs of all the professors who had not resigned be vacated, whereupon all of the professors did resign. The reconstituted faculty consisted of the same three full-time professors and nine lecturers, but the Chancellor stepped into the role of acting dean for one year. Dr. J. P. Gordy, professor of the History of Education, followed the Chancellor and served as acting dean from 1902 to 1904.

In 1904 Dr. Thomas M. Balliet, of Springfield, Massachusetts, was named dean of the School of Pedagogy. Dr. Balliet had done graduate work at Yale and at Leipzig, and he had been superintendent of schools at Springfield, Massachusetts. He served as dean of the School of Pedagogy until his retirement in 1919. During its last year, 1920–21, the School again operated under an acting dean, Marshall S. Brown, dean of the faculties. A strong administrative organization of the teacher-education unit at New York University was still to be achieved.

With the exception of the incident in 1900, the record contains nothing of a specifically negative nature. Neither are there evidences of strong, positive pronouncements, ideas, or actions. It would appear that the personnel of the School of Pedagogy manifested interest in contributing to the improvement of teacher qualifications, but that they had to carry out their responsibilities under the handicaps of unclarified policies and practices and with extremely limited physical facilities.

STAFF AND FACILITIES

The three professors constituting the first full-time faculty of the School of Pedagogy began their work in the Gothic building on the east side of Washington Square. This group included Dean Allen, Edgar D. Shimer, who had taught the first courses in pedagogy between 1887 and 1890, and Edgar R. Shaw. Allen taught *History of Educational Thought* and *Methodology*, Shimer offered *Philosophy of Education* and *Educational Psychology*, and Shaw's course was entitled *Critical Examination of the Literature of Education.* In addition, Addison B. Poland lectured on *Didactics* and *Applied Pedagogy*, and E. H. Cook taught *School Economy* and *School Law*.

During the early years of the institution the faculty included two professors who went on to achieve outstanding reputations in the field of education. One of these was Charles H. Judd, who was a staff member between 1898 and 1901. Dr. Judd made significant contributions in the field of intelligence testing and educational measurement and eventually became head of the School of Education of the University of Chicago. The other notable member of the faculty was Nicholas Murray Butler, who was to culminate a distinguished career in education as president of Columbia University. In the two years Mr. Butler was with the University of the City of New York, he made two significant recommendations for the expansion of the emerging teacher-education profession. He presented to the administration of Columbia College a plan to offer instruction in pedagogies as an elective for undergraduates, both men and women, not necessarily matriculants of Columbia College. Mr. Butler estimated that there would be as many as two hundred persons—most of them women —eager for such work.[3] The Trustees of Columbia, however, were not able to discern any advantage likely to ensue to Columbia College which could be taken as an offset to the confusion resulting from such a plan, and they rejected the idea.

A second scheme is revealed through a series of letters exchanged between Vice-Chancellor MacCracken, of the University of the City of New York, and President Seth Low, of Columbia, proposing a federation between the School of Pedagogy and Columbia College. Once again this proved to be an abortive effort, and late in 1889 Nicholas Murray Butler opened the New York College for the Training of Teachers in the shadow of Washington Square. He thereupon severed his connection with the University of the City of New York. Within ten years the Trustees of Columbia University capitulated and But-

[3] *Annual Report* of the President and Treasurer of Columbia University, 1929, p. 51.

ler's school was incorporated into Columbia University as Teachers College.

In the ensuing years the pedagogical faculty included several members whose offerings represented pioneer efforts to broaden the scope of teacher education. Among these, the following may be mentioned: Dr. Abraham A. Brill, who offered some of the first courses in elementary and advanced psychoanalysis, and Henry H. Goddard, who introduced pedagogical consideration of the defective child. Brill was recognized as Freud's official translator, and Goddard had translated the original scale devised by Binet. Goddard later became director of research at the Training School for Backward and Feebleminded Children, at Vineland, New Jersey.

The reputation of the School of Pedagogy was enhanced by the addition of Dr. Paul Rankov Radosavljevich, an early leader in experimental education, and Dr. Herman Harrel Horne, an accepted authority in the philosophy of education. Radosavljevich had studied and worked with the celebrated Ernest Meumann, the pioneer in educational experimentation at the University of Zurich. Horne, ardent exponent of the philosophy of idealism, achieved recognition as critical interpreter of John Dewey.

On the distaff side, the faculty included Annie L. Jessup, whose courses in home economics were among the first to be included in a teacher-training program at the university level, and Harriet Melissa Mills, the early leader in the kindergarten movement who brought that aspect of early childhood education to the program of the School of Pedagogy.

TABLE I
FACULTY STRUCTURE
SCHOOL OF PEDAGOGY
1890–1920

Year	Dean	Prof.	Assoc. Profs.	Asst. Profs.	Instruct's	Lect'rs	Un-desig.	Tot.
1890–91	Allen	3	1			1	1	6
1891–92	"	2	1			3		6
1892–93	"	4				1		5
1893–94	Shaw	3				2		5
1894–95	"	2	1			2	1	6
1895–96	"	2				2		4
1896–97	"	7				3		10
1897–98	"	7				7		16
1898–99	"	6				8		15
1899–00	"	6				8		16
1900–01	MacCracken (Acting)	6				8		17
1901–02	"	6				9		17
1902–03	"	6			4	7		19
1903–04	Gordy (Acting)	7	1		5			14
1904–05	Balliet	6			8	5		15
1905–06	"	6			8	7		16
1906–07	"	6			3	10		18
1907–08	"	8	2		3	9		17
1908–09	"	8	1			14		22
1909–10	"	8	1	2		14		22
1910–11	"	8	2	3	3	9		17
1911–12	"	5	2	2	5	14		24
1912–13	"	5			5	14		27
1913–14	"	6			3	3		31
1914–15	"	6			6	11		48
1915–16	"	7			3	2	16	22
1916–17	"	5	1	1	4	8	21	26
1917–18	"	5	1		4	3	11	23
1918–19	"	5	1		7	5	13	19
1919–20	M. Brown (Acting)	5				6	9	

Using the data of Table 1, page 24, the data indicate little change in terms of additions to the professorial staff between 1900 and the final year of the School. In fact, the number of full professorships diminishes after 1910, picks up very slightly between 1913 and 1916, and then levels off to five between 1916 and 1920. A slight rise in the categories of associate professor and assistant professor is noted. The greatest changes in numbers occur in the categories of instructor and lecturer. In the case of the former, these represented primarily persons borrowed from other units of the University as program expansion required staff from such specialized areas as commercial education. The same situation is true for the category of lecturer where persons were drafted, either from within the University or from commerce and industry, to teach specialized courses in technical and vocational education as these areas became part of the secondary school curriculum and the demand for teachers of these objects grew.

The persistent absence of adequate funds plagued the School's officials in the matter of building a faculty as it did on other questions of expansion. This may be assumed to be responsible, in part, for the excess of part-time over full-time personnel. On the other hand, for many of the newer areas of instruction, especially in technological and industrial education, college teachers of these subjects were not available, and it was necessary to draft practitioners to get the training of teachers under way.

Between 1890 and 1920, cultural forces whose impact on higher education would come to full fruition in the twentieth century were appearing on the horizon. These forces touched the elementary level in connection with a growing concern for the handicapped child and particularly the secondary school which was expanding its role to include preparation for a vocation as well as preparation for college. In turn, these forces became determinants in teacher education.

Thus, by 1920 the School of Pedagogy numbered among its faculty experts in the education of backward and defective children, specialists in the theoretical side of the teaching-learning process, and artisans from trade and industry who were concerned with the practical arts and skills now called for in American life. Together they were pioneering in the professionalization of an indigenous pedagogy for a democracy.

It may be assumed that the optimum effectiveness of the teaching staff was influenced by the handicaps under which it labored, namely, little voice in planning, inadequate funds, and, added to these, extremely limited facilities.

Facilities

The exact amount of space allotted to the School of Pedagogy for administrative duties and conduct of the program is not recorded. It is known that the University officials rented the upper two floors of the four-story Gothic building to a bohemian colony of artists and writers. These tenants included two who brought enduring fame to the University, for here John W. Draper conducted his experiments in photography resulting in the first complete portrait of the human face. Furthermore, he made significant contributions to Samuel F. B. Morse's development of the telegraph, which was completed in the late 1830s in one of the University buildings. This left two floors to be shared by the University College (until its removal to University Heights in 1894); the School of Law; the Graduate Division; and the School of Pedagogy.

In 1892, in response to efforts of the Women's Advisory Committee, three additional rooms were assigned to the work in pedagogy. Also, the use of the chapel and the mathematics room at stipulated hours was authorized, and a fourth room made available provided the Women's Advisory Committee could secure the necessary furniture and fixtures.

Two years later the gray stone structure gave way to a ten-story modern brick building occupying not only the original site, but two adjacent lots on Waverly Place. The American Book Company rented the first seven floors of the new building. The top floor was used for offices of the central University administration. The Graduate Division (which became the Graduate School of Arts and Science in 1896), the School of Law, and the School of Pedagogy occupied the eighth and ninth floors. The facilities of the School of Pedagogy crowded into this space included the office of the dean, the library, the psychological laboratory, recitation rooms, and "the cloak rooms for men and women respectively." The school had a large and well-equipped library to which the latest pedagogical works were constantly added.

It is a matter of record that, throughout his years of service in the School of Pedagogy and later in the School of Education, Professor Radosavljevich made a monthly contribution for the purchase of books and other library materials. This gesture was made over a span of thirty-six years. Upon his retirement in 1945, Dr. Radosavljevich presented his personal library to New York University as a memorial to Dean Balliet. The collection was named the Balliet Teacher's Library.

No record can be found of any specialized equipment which the psychology laboratory might have contained or which might have been used in connection with other courses such as the one entitled *Woodwork for Teachers of Backward and Defective Children.*

Certain professional organizations also used the facilities of the School as their headquarters. Among these were The Society of Pedagogical Research, the New York University Society of Child Study, the Alumni Association of Doctors of Pedagogy, the Suburban Council of Education, and the Society for the Comparative Study of Pedagogy.

The quarters in this building housed the School of Pedagogy for the next twenty-five years and, in them, served several hundreds of students annually.

STUDENT BODY

Perhaps as perplexing as the early financial problems of the University, if not more so, was the decision as to who should be admitted to the new academic unit. The original intention, as reflected in the Chancellor's reports, was to make this a graduate school and offer only the master's and doctor's degrees. But the constant refinement of license requirements and the incentive to improve their status—financially and professionally—sent hundreds of teachers to the doors of the School of Pedagogy, anxious to undertake advanced pedagogical training.

It soon became apparent, therefore, that the original plan would not be feasible, since in an initial group of two hundred applicants only fifty were college graduates. It was decided that to deny these teachers the self-improvement they so eagerly sought would not be a constructive solution, and a classification of auditor was set up to accommodate these non-graduates. This by no means solved the problem, for within a decade, several hundred local teachers and principals were demanding the opportunity to take such courses as would make them eligible for the bachelor's degree. A further complication arose in the fact that those who were college graduates persisted in earning the doctor of philosophy degree granted by the Graduate School, rather than the doctor of pedagogy conferred by the School of Pedagogy.

In 1903 graduation from a recognized college was made a condition of matriculation in the teacher-education unit, and the Collegiate Division was organized to make it possible for graduates of normal schools, or those who had completed two years of college work, to complete the last two years of work for the undergraduate degree.

Conditions for admission to the School of Pedagogy, and its degree requirements were as follows:

Catalogue N.Y.U. 1896–97

Pg. 161

Auditors

In addition to those who are candidates for degrees, a second class of students may be enrolled, to be known as auditors. To this class may be admitted all such as commend themselves to the Faculty as prepared to receive benefit from the lectures, but such students cannot be candidates for a degree. They may attend the lectures as the faculty may direct, upon payment of $10 for *each course* attended; but the privilege of seminary work is not extended to them, and they are not admitted to examinations.

Pg. 162

DEGREES
Doctor of Pedagogy

The degree of Doctor of Pedagogy will be conferred upon a student who has met the following conditions:

I. He must have been credited with attendance upon the required lectures and seminaries.

II. He must have successfully completed the five Major and the five Minor courses. The Minor courses marked with an asterisk (*) are elective; the student is required to choose one of these in making up his list of Minor courses.

III. He must have presented the prescribed thesis as defined hereafter, and have received approval of the same.

IV. He must either have presented a certificate showing four years successful experience in school-room work, or he must have taught two years under the direction of the Faculty and with such success as to receive their approval.

V. He must have paid the fee of $20 for each Major course, and $10 for each Minor course required.

Pg. 162

Master of Pedagogy

The degree of Master of Pedagogy will be conferred upon a student who has met the following conditions:

I. He must have been credited with attendance upon the required lectures and seminaries.

II. He must have successfully completed four courses, three of which must be Major courses.

III. He must either have presented a certificate showing two years successful experience in teaching, or he must have taught one year under the direction of the Faculty and with such success as to receive their approval.

IV. He must have paid the fee of $20 for each Major course, and $10 for each Minor course required.

Pg. 370

New York University
Catalogue
1911–12

CONDITIONS OF ADMISSION AND MATRICULATION

In June, 1903, by vote of the Faculty, graduation from a recognized college of Arts and Science, or its equivalent, was made a condition of matriculation for either the degree of Master of Pedagogy or that of Doctor of Pedagogy. Students not candidates for either degree are admitted on a lower standard. More specifically stated, these requirements are as follows:

(a) Graduates of recognized Colleges of Arts and Science may matriculate as candidates for degrees, without examination, on presentation of their college diploma.

(b) All teachers of experience and all graduates of state or city normal schools are admitted, without examination, but are not matriculated as candidates for a degree. Such students, if their attendance is regular and they pass successfully the required examinations, receive a certificate for the courses completed. Upon presentation of these certificates the Board of Education of New York City will give credit for the courses named in them under certain conditions specified by the Board.

(c) Students,* whether college graduates or not, who do

---

*Some of the most advanced students of the School of Pedagogy belong to this class. They hold prominent positions as principals or superintendents and attend lectures irregularly or when their professional duties permit.

not wish to attend regularly or receive credit for their work, are admitted as special students and are not required to pass examinations.

Students who wish to be candidates for degrees, or who desire credit for the courses which they take, must enroll not later than October 21 for the work of the first term.

Persons whose academic training does not extend beyond that of the public high school or academy, and who have had neither professional training nor experience in teaching, are not admitted.

(d) Graduates of approved State Normal Schools (of equal rank with those of Class I of the Board of Regents), and persons who have completed the work of the Freshman and Sophomore years in a recognized college, may enter the Washington Square Collegiate Division,* complete the last two years of the college course, receive their degree, and then matriculate in the School of Pedagogy and become candidates for its degrees.

Pg. 371

New York University
Catalogue

REQUIREMENTS FOR THE MASTER'S DEGREE

Fourteen hours of class-room work per week for the University year is the minimum requirement for the degree of Master of Pedagogy (Pd. M.). These hours must include Courses 116, 201, 206, 301, together with six additional hours to be elected with the approval of the Dean, at least two of which must be in Advanced Courses.

In addition to the successful completion of these courses, the student must present a certificate showing two years successful experience in teaching. A high degree of scholarship is required in all courses taken.

Candidates for this degree must file written application not

---

* A special circular describing the courses in the Collegiate Division may be obtained by addressing the Secretary, Professor James E. Lough, New York University, Washington Square, New York.

later than May 1, preceding the commencement at which the conferring of the degree is sought.

REQUIREMENTS FOR THE DOCTOR'S DEGREE

In addition to the master's degree eleven hours of classroom work per week for the University year is required for the degree of Doctor of Pedagogy (Pd. D.). These hours must include two hours in Special Method in Group IV, and at least six hours of Advanced Courses, distributed as follows: in Group I, two hours; Group II, two hours; and in Group III, two hours. The remaining three hours are elective.

In addition to the successful completion of these courses, the student must present a certificate showing three years' successful experience in teaching. A high degree of scholarship is required in all courses taken.

Candidates for this degree are also required to attend such seminars as the Faculty may appoint.

These degrees, held by college graduates, are recognized by the New York Board of Education as equivalent to the corresponding degrees of Master of Arts and Doctor of Philosophy, held by college graduates.

THESIS FOR THE DOCTORATE

For the degree of Doctor of Pedagogy, a Thesis, to be known as the "Thesis for the Doctorate in Pedagogy," must be delivered to the Secretary of the Faculty *not later than the first Monday in April* preceding the Commencement at which the conferring of the degree is sought. The subject for this Thesis must be presented to the Faculty for its approval before the third Saturday of October of the same academic year. This Thesis must show original treatment, or give evidence of independent research. The Thesis must include an analytical table of contents and a bibliography of the subject, and must be arranged according to a pattern which may be seen in the library of the School.

It will be noted in these materials that in 1911 the term "special student" superseded that of auditor. This was necessitated by the practice in the School of Pedagogy of inviting holders of the doctor's degree to audit further courses as guests of the institution. Special students were disbarred from seminars but could attend all other lectures. They could not be candidates for degrees.

In the beginning, the officers of administration and the faculty apparently were of the persuasion that book learning was not all that went into the making of a teacher. In addition to the course work required, candidates for the master of pedagogy had to present evidence of two years of successful teaching experience or complete one year of satisfactory teaching under the direction of the faculty. Those seeking the doctor of pedagogy degree had to show four years of such teaching or complete two years of teaching under faculty direction. The School of Pedagogy would appear to have instituted the concept of student teaching as early as 1896. However, without a recorded explanation, in 1911 the required teaching experience was lowered to three years for the doctoral candidate and no further reference to student teaching appears until after the formal establishment of the School of Education.

Table II, pages 36–37, presents the annual enrollment for the School of Pedagogy between 1890 and 1920. From these figures it will be seen that men exceeded women in only six of these years, except in the case of the auditor or special student groups where the situation was always reversed.

The abnormally high enrollment in 1898–99 was due to the proposal by the New York City superintendent of schools to condition the advancement of teachers upon their taking courses in pedagogical instruction. He suggested that such courses be accepted for licensing without examination. The state legislature did not support this proposal, and the effect of the decision was reflected in the enrollment for the following year.

However, the comment of the Chancellor regarding the situation was, "Our School will be none the worse on account of this. We are aiming to make a center of pedagogical influence for the United States rather than for New York City." [4]

Possibly with a view to attracting students from other sections of the country, scholarships were made available (once again aided and abetted by the Women's Advisory Committee), with some unique conditions of eligibility. For example, the Western and Southwestern Fellowships of $5000 each, were open respectively only to teachers along the lines of the Missouri, Pacific, and Iron Mountain Railways and those along the lines of the Texas, Pacific, St. Louis Southwestern, and International and Great Northern Railways. The record indicates that the winner of the fellowship received the interest on the principal annually. The total principal of these scholarships and fellowships amounted to $36,500. In addition there was an announcement of five temporary scholarships covering the entire cost of tuition for one year.

For 1910–11 and 1911–12 the excessive number of males represents matriculants in the Graduate School of Arts and Science who took the pedagogical courses in order to qualify for teaching licenses.

No consistent pattern of growth is discernible from an examination of the data of Table II, pages 36–37. In fact,

[4] *Annual Report* of the Chancellor of the University Council, 1899, p. 72.

TABLE II

ANNUAL ENROLLMENT—SCHOOL OF PEDAGOGY
1890–1920

Year	Degree Candidates			Auditors and/or Special Students			Grand Total
	Men	Women	Total	Men	Women	Total	
1890–91	20	30	50	59	105	164	214
1891–92	48	144	192	8	26	34	226
1892–93	44	79	123	3	8	11	134
1893–94	23	45	68	2	8	10	78
1894–95	20	45	65	2	8	10	75
1895–96	28	51	79	3	9	12	91
1896–97	55	47	102	5	10	15	117
1897–98	61	92	153	7	26	33	186
1898–99	58	257	315	9	14	23	338
1899–00	64	188	252	7	12	19	271
1900–01	70	93	163	9	32	41	204
1901–02	101	152	253	6	23	29	282
1902–03	105	129	234	7	28	35	269
1903–04	110	86	196	26	78	104	300
1904–05	101	76	177	29	100	129	306
1905–06	93	102	195	13	77	90	285
1906–07	77	212	289	36	56	92	381
1907–08	98	164	262	60	118	178	440
1908–09	87	148	235	24	60	84	319

TABLE II (Cont.)

Year	Degree Candidates			Auditors and/or Special Students			Grand Total
	Men	Women	Total	Men	Women	Total	
1909–10	94	159	247	33	50	83	330
1910–11	60	82	142	105	158	263	405(a)
1911–12	118	29	147	76	162	238	385(b), (c)
1912–13	72	40	112	23	121	144	256
1913–14	92	180	272	42	112	154	426
1914–15	90	76	166	41	88	129	295
1915–16	88	338	426	47	43	90	516 (d)
1916–17	18	30	48	75	100	175	223
1917–18	30	34	64	70	100	170	234
1918–19	18	26	44	44	46	90	134
1919–20	19	28	47	55	66	121	168(e)

(a) Includes 163 students from Graduate School of Arts and Science
(b)   "   142   "   "   "   "   "   "   "
(c)   "   23 special students in Domestic Art
(d)   "   38 from Graduate School and 52 from Washington Square College
(e)   "   47   "   "   "   "   52 from   "   "   "

they present an extremely erratic picture. The sharp drop in enrollment, from 516 in 1915–16 to 168 in 1919–20, would suggest the operation of some unusual circumstances. Among the factors influencing college enrollments in these years was, of course, America's entry into World War I. This not only affected male enrollments, but also the enrollment of women, since many left teaching to go into various kinds of war work. Also, as had been previously noted, the student body was made up largely of school teachers from New York City and the metropolitan area.

In time, the establishment of two municipal teacher-training institutions (Jamaica, in Queens, and Maxwell, in Brooklyn) affected the enrollment in the School of Pedagogy. This condition was further aggravated by the availability of courses through the New York City Board of Education which were recognized for alertness credit toward advancement for teachers in service. Such courses were offered either free or at nominal cost.

By 1919, although there were still 121 special students, the number of degree candidates had fallen to forty-seven. This did not seem auspicious for a professional degree-granting school within a university structure, and it led to a serious concern on the part of the administrative officers regarding the future of the division. On numerous occasions, the dean noted the fact that a privately endowed school could not compete for students with institutions which had municipal or state treasuries behind them. He reaffirmed the need for the School of Pedagogy to make its appeal to the entire country.

Nevertheless, in its time the halls of the School of Pedagogy echoed to the discussions of individuals who went on to achieve prominance in their chosen fields. They became outstanding teachers, principals, superintendents of schools, and members of the New York City Board of Examiners. Such alumni included Joseph Abelson, Jacob Greenberg, Julia Richman, Joseph Jablonower, and Jacob Theobald, to cite but a few.

The professional success of the men and women who constituted the student body of the School of Pedagogy in some measure was dependent upon the program of instruction they received in the teacher-education unit of New York University.

THE PROGRAM

As early as 1899, a basic conception of professional education was laid down which included four goals: general culture, special scholarship, professional knowledge, and technical skill.

The construction of a program to meet these objectives was no small matter. First, the men engaged in the task were themselves largely products of liberal arts colleges. While they sought to break away from a portion of the classical curriculum and bring to the students the latest knowledges of the field of pedagogy, this was not always readily achieved. It has been noted that a restraining influence was the lack of complete autonomy of the faculty and administration of the School of Pedagogy to formulate its own policies and program. The announced outlines of instruction reveal an attempt to achieve a combination of the old and new throughout the years the School was in operation. Some idea of the effort made in this direction can be judged from the catalogue description of a course entitled *Standard Classical Authors*. The potential student was informed that the course would require a careful study of: (1) Xenophon's *Cyropaedia* and *Memorabilia*; (2) Plato's *Apology, Crito, Phaedo,* and *The Republic*; (3) Aristotle's *Rhetoric, Ethics,* and *Politics*; (4) Cicero's *De Oratore*; (5) Quintillian's *Interests of Oratory*; (6) Plutarch's *On the Education of Children*; (7) Rousseau's *Emile*; (8) Pestalozzi's *Leonard and Gertrude* and *Evening Hours of a Hermit*; and (9) Locke, *On Education*, Milton's *Tractate on Education* (edited by Browning), and Montaigne's *Essays on Pedantism* (sic) and on the *Institution and Education of Children*.

The influence of several cultural components may be discerned in reviewing the program in teacher education throughout the decades between 1890 and 1920. First, as has been reported, it was intended that the work be given on the graduate level. From the outset, the faculty found it difficult to reconcile the advanced caliber of instruction with the heterogeneous character of the student body. Secondly, the mass of information growing out of the extensive work being done in psychology and measurement was constantly having to be modified as research and experimentation brought new findings. This required a continual adjustment of instructional materials to accommodate new data.

The rising pragmatism was another factor which compelled educators to formulate a new philosophy of education attuned to the practical demands of a growing industrial society. Faced with these dynamics, the instructor had the responsibility of keeping himself and his teaching materials abreast of pedagogical developments in his field. In part, this approach may suggest a major distinction between teacher training at the university level and that found in the normal schools. Referring to the latter institution, William S. Elsbree, in his book *The American Teacher: Evolution of a Profession in a Democracy*, has commented that no two courses of study appear to have been alike. He presents some idea of what normal-school offerings were like in 1890 in this illustration:

Course of Study in Castine Normal School, Maine, 1890

F CLASS	E CLASS	D CLASS
Arithmetic, from percentage	Arithmetic, methods,	Alegebra Geometry
Grammer	Grammar	Physics
Geography	Geography	Physical Geography
School economy	Algebra	
Reading	Physiology	Drawing
Writing, one-half term		
Elementary music, one-half term		

Course of Study (continued)
Second Year

C CLASS	B CLASS	A CLASS
Geometry	Psychology	Didactics and history of education
General History	Chemistry	
Physics	United States History	tion
Rhetoric		Practice teaching
Botany	Civil government	English literature
Bookkeeping, one-half term	Moral philosophy	Astronomy
	Practice teaching	Geology, one-half term

Much of the above appears closer to the work of the high school rather than representing post-secondary education. From its inception, the program of the School of Pedagogy displayed an attempt to provide a broader and more professional type of preparation for teaching.

Since there is a noticeable change in the number and types of courses offered in the School of Pedagogy following 1910, the discussion of this topic is presented in two parts: between the year of its founding and 1910 and from this latter date through its terminal year 1920.

Course Offerings Between 1890–1910

Students of graduate pedagogy were expected to complete two types of courses for the graduate degrees conferred by the School of Pedagogy, namely, master of pedagogy and doctor of pedagogy. The classical, traditional, liberal arts subjects intended to foster culture and scholarship, and the pedagogical courses intended to provide the tools necessary for effective teaching.

While the humanities were retained in the total programs of the School of Pedagogy throughout its tenure, such courses were taught first by the faculty of the Graduate Division (who had their official appointments in the undergraduate University College of Arts and Science), later through the Collegiate Division (1903–12), and eventually through the undergraduate liberal arts college at Washington Square (Washington Square College). This meant that, between 1890 and 1920, students in the School of Pedagogy had to get a portion of their program in a division other than the one in which they were matriculated and with a faculty outside the school of their choice.

Pedagogical Studies Prior to 1910

The total number of courses offered in the School of Pedagogy rose from eleven in 1890 to forty-six in 1910. Courses in psychology increased from twenty to twenty-five percent of the program by 1910. In the scientific aspects of the new pedagogy—that is, those areas of study concerned with tests, measurement, and experiment in education—the administration of the teacher-training division manifested a cautious but distinct intention that these new disciplines should be included. For example, in its first year of formal organization, the School listed courses entitled *Anatomy, Physiology,* and *Hygiene* and *Experimental and Practical Work.* By 1900 the following were added: *Physiological Pedagogics: Relation of Medicine to Pedagogy, The Practical Applications of the Psychology of Expressional Activities,* and *A Critical Study of Kindergarten Activities.* The catalogue for 1904–05 carries a group of courses headed "Practice of Teaching" with the first introduction of clearly identified methods courses. Before the end of its second decade, the School offered *Physiography, The Physical Nature of the Child, Anthropological Study of School Children, Observation,* and *Experimental Pedagogy.*

It may be assumed that the appearance of courses relating to the psychological and scientific study of child behavior grew out of the advances in understanding child development spearheaded in the United States by G. Stanley Hall. The focus of teaching shifted to the student, based on the assertion that no education could be worthy, much less efficient, that persisted in ignoring his needs and his development. These progressive approaches to teaching-learning theories were to exert their influence on teaching and teacher education for the next three decades.

Administration as an area of academic concern was introduced in the first year of the School's operation with the inclusion of two such courses. While this number was increased to four courses in 1900, the administrative aspects of education did not receive full consideration until after 1920. A course in *Research in Educational Problems* is found among the offerings by 1905. While one methods course is listed for 1890 and five for 1905, again it was after 1910 that such courses showed an appreciable increase.

The interesting elements in the program up to 1910 relate to inclusion of such new fields as art, music, and domestic art which were not commonly found in teacher-training curricula up to this time.

The rate of acceleration in the field of pedagogy and the degree to which the educationists were carried away by their enthusiasm, can be glimpsed in the descriptions of two courses offered in neighboring institutions in New York City. The first of these is labeled: Household Arts 67b *Institutional Laundries*. Its description stated:

This course is intended for persons preparing to become managers of institutional laundries. It considers their planning and equipment and methods of management, including such topics as machine versus hand work; the typical laundry apparatus, soap, starches, and other materials; methods of handling different fabrics; staff and financial management. Machine practice in the laundry laboratory is included and opportunities for observation and practice in an institutional laundry.[5]

In an entirely different vein was a course entitled *The Institutes of Education* which had the following description:

This course is comprised under the following heads:
1. An examination of the commonly accepted principles and maxims of education to determine their scope and limits. 2. The educative values of the different subjects of study, and to what extent these values are determined by mode of presentation. 3. The coordination of subjects. 4. Incentives. 5. School hygiene, including school buildings, grounds, lighting, heating, ventilation, furniture, sanitation, physical training, fatigue, school diseases.
Students will be required to make tests of ventilation in certain accesible schools, determining by means of the anemometer the number of cubic feet of air entering the room per minute for each pupil, the number of cubic feet passing out, the temperature and humidity of the air of the room, the impurity as denoted by the proportionate amount of carbonic acid gas present. 6. School organization, management and supervision. 7. Child study, involving observation, tests, and measurements to determine intellectual, physical and moral differences and tendencies. 8. Will training. 9. A study of De Garmo's 'Essentials of Method.' Everett's 'Science of Thought,' Lange's 'Apperception,' etc. 10. The relation of induction and deduction to the various subjects of study in schools. 11. The present status and tendency of manual training. 12. Methods of teaching subjects in elementary and secondary schools, Reading, Writing, Spelling, Number and Arithmetic, Geography, Form Study and Drawing, Elementary Science, History, English Composition, Physiology, Algebra, Inventional Astronomy, Rhetoric, English Literature, etc. with required presentation of lessons for criticism and discussion. 13. Reading and discussion of Rosenkranz's 'Philos-

[5] *Announcement,* Teachers College, Columbia University, 1910–11, p. 109.

ophy of Education.' During the year the students will visit certain schools of high rank in New York City and vicinity for observation and study. The work of this course will be by lectures and seminaria. Opportunity will be afforded for special investigation and study of the teaching of a chosen subject.[6]

Whether or not this description overawed prospective teachers cannot be determined. The record reveals, however, that for this year the enrollment dropped to 134 students as against 214 in the previous year. The variety of items to be covered, as listed in this description, might also lend support to the assumption that the topics were treated generally rather than thoroughly and critically.

After the turn of the century influences of the rising pragmatism can be seen in a noticeable shift to the more practical aspects of education. As early as 1906–07 courses were offered in industrial arts, physical training and school hygiene, and, as previously stated, domestic art. Further innovations were to come during the next decade.

Program of the School of Pedagogy 1910–20

While work in the humanities was retained in the pedagogical curricula, there are observable variations in both amount and content. Such courses as *History of Education, History of Philosophy, Logic, Ethics,* and *Educational Classics* remained constants; other types of liberal arts courses in art, music and social studies appeared sporadically. The proportion of the total program devoted to the liberal arts subjects ranges from thirty-two percent in 1912–13 to ten percent in 1916–17. In the last year of

[6] *Catalogue* University of the City of New York, 1892–93, section relating to School of Pedagogy, pp. 84–85.

the School of Pedagogy this figure was nineteen percent. Students were still required to go outside the School of Pedagogy for this portion of the program.

The field of psychology, in all its refinements, continued to occupy a prominent place in the curriculum. As early as 1915–16 elementary and advanced courses in psychoanalysis were offered. The distinction between child and adolescent psychology was recognized, and work covering genetic through experimental psychology was found in the course listings. In addition, reference was made to a psychological laboratory ". . . supplied with the ordinary psychological apparatus, the equipment having special reference to problems which have a direct bearing on pedagogy."

The description of the course entitled *Physiological and Experimental Psychology* reflects response to the child development movement. It included the statement:

The aim of the course is to enable the student to understand the rapidly increasing literature of child study and of psychological investigations as applied to educational problems . . . to recognize the limits and possibilities of this line of work, and to enable him to make future investigations which shall have value to psychology and to pedagogy.

Despite indications of difficulties ahead, one manifestation being the decreasing enrollment, new and sometimes original types of learning opportunities continued to be announced. For example, retailing as an area of formal study was offered in 1917–18 through such courses as *Business Organization and Merchandising, Educational Methods for the Department Store, Store Systems and*

Salesmanship, Textile Departments and Non-Textile Merchandise, and *Non-Textile Departments.*

Methods courses became firmly entrenched in the School's program after 1910. The work relating to the education of backward and defective children illustrated a response to social pressures for a more humane understanding of the handicapped and underprivileged. While work in administration and supervision was introduced, these areas were given greater momentum in succeeding eras. Finally, the fields of vocational education, commercial education, and elementary and secondary education gave signs of responding to the progressive movement in education after 1917.

RESUMÉ OF PROGRAM

Table IV, page 130, indicates an erratic pattern of growth in the number of courses offered in the teacher-training division of New York University. Beginning with only eleven courses in 1890, the number reached forty-nine in 1910, remained at forty-four for the next two years, and then reached a peak of sixty-one in 1913–14. For three years following 1913–14 there is a fluctuating loss in number of offerings. Although the full complement of sixty-one courses was restored in 1917–18, this was true only for that year. For 1918–19 and 1919–20 the total offerings numbered thirty-two courses.

Reasons for these fluctuations are not too easily identified. However, in all probability four conditions may be assumed to have had some impact on the situation: First, the fact that the School of Pedagogy was still in a period of trial and error and still experimenting with program organization; secondly, the erratic enrollment picture would suggest a relationship to the number of courses offered. Another influence was the availability of pedagogical instruction, recognized by the New York City Board of Education, where tuition was not involved. Finally, World War I undoubtedly affected the School of Pedagogy in several ways—in loss of staff, in loss of enrollment, and, in turn, in loss of income.

Entry into New Fields

The period from 1910 through 1920 saw the development of four major fields of study: (1) special education, (2) experimental pedagogy, (3) commercial education, and (4) industrial education.

Of the work in special education, in his annual report for 1913–14, the dean wrote: "This University was among the first to take up the question of training teachers for the various types of backward and defective children for which special classes are now organized in many cities."
He further noted that the University originally embarked upon work in this field under the leadership of the Women's Advisory Committee. This is the last official reference to this committee.

Radosavljevich, working in experimental pedagogy, combined the new evaluative measures with some of the first attempts to relate anthropological data to the study of individual differences and the effects of these differences on the learning process.

The introduction of commercial education served two purposes: to train individuals for business and industry and to prepare teachers of these subjects. To this end a plan was worked out for the utilization of staff members from the School of Commerce to teach these courses. By 1920 however, there was a separation of courses intended for those going into industry and those going into education. Thereafter, the former work was offered exclusively in the School of Commerce, Accounts and Finance. Methodology was handled in the School of Pedagogy.

The School responded to a growing emphasis on vocational education as manfested by governmental supportive action. While industrial arts education was stressed, two courses relating to the structure and function of vocational education were introduced. Although this represented only a token response to a demand which became increasingly insistent during the 1920s, it does imply alertness on the part of the leadership of the School to changing emphases in education, especially at the secondary level.

The institution appears to have branched out into fields not commonly included in the programs of normal schools or teachers colleges. For example, prior to 1910 a single course in the teaching of music was offered. Out of this grew a Department of Music Education which in 1913 listed nine courses. Again, in 1911 innovations in such programs were noted by the addition of two courses: one, *Methods of Teaching Modern Languages,* and the other entitled *The Teaching of Art.* However, these special courses and departments with few exceptions had to be discontinued after the disintegrating effects of World War I.

The program of the School of Pedagogy manifested

some lag in responding to the expanded needs of secondary education. In its final year, except for the content work in commercial education, the only listings under the heading "secondary education" were methods courses for specific subjects such as *Teaching of Bookkeeping, Teaching of Commercial and Economic Geography, Teaching of Algebra in High School,* and *Teaching of General Science.* There appears to have been an absence of courses implying study of the structure and function of the high school as an educational entity.

Awareness of these and other weaknesses is indicated by Dean Balliet in his last report to the Chancellor. He stated that three major needs of the institution (aside from its fundamental financial needs) were: (1) need of a strong department of secondary education in which the emphasis would be placed on the practical side of administration and methods of teaching, (2) need of a department of general school administration for the training of superintendents, principals and other supervisory officers, and (3) greater emphasis on supervision of instruction, which area, he wrote, ". . . is today the weakest point in public schools."

Balliet further anticipated the trend toward a greater degree of specialization in teacher-education institutions. He pointed out that pedagogy was rapidly becoming so large a subject, dealing with problems requiring exceptional training in psychology, sociology, and other related fields, that the grade teacher could not be expected to master it.

Between 1890 and 1920 changes are evident in the program of the School of Pedagogy both in the extent of the work offered and the nature of it. Over these thirty years certain strengths and weaknesses in these efforts may be discerned.

Strengths

The program required of students preparing to teach always included studies from the academic subjects as well as from pedagogical disciplines.

As training for teachers of such subjects as music, art, domestic art, industrial education, and commercial subjects became available and as techniques for teaching the handicapped were developed, new professional opportunities in teaching opened up.

Operating with inadequate staff and facilities, the School neverthless pioneered in such fields as special education and experimental pedagogy, incorporating in its courses utilization of the expanding pedagogical knowledge.

Through the work available in the first teacher-training unit at New York University, some contributions may be assumed to have been made to the improvements in qualifications of teachers, both prospective and in service, and to the further improvement and development of the teaching profession.

Weaknesses

With no clearly defined curricula, there was a minimum of distinction in preparation for various educational services. This was especially true in the case of teachers for the elementary or for the secondary schools. The latter area received only cursory attention late in the School's existence, and in the case of the former, emphasis seems to have been put on service to the handicapped child with reference in only one year (1910–11) to the education of the preschool child.

There is no discernible pattern of courses which would make obvious a developmental plan built on a basic philosophy of teacher education.

In the light of the rapidly changing characteristics of public education, the innovations tried by the faculty and administration of the first teacher-training unit at New York University may be said to have been too little and too late. Once again, conditions were changing faster on the cultural scene than they were in the educational, and this lag tended to weaken the impact of the first graduate work in pedagogy available at the university level.

It should be kept in mind that such weaknesses as those enumerated above were not unique to the institution under discussion, since the record of the period includes very little systematic consideration of the purposes of teacher education from the point of view of the needs of the profession.

A partial explanation of this may be found in an examination of the socio-cultural forces impinging on education in the years immediately preceding the reorganization of the School of Pedagogy.

SUMMARY

In summary, it may be stated that the initial teacher-education unit at New York University had a parent body whose founders gave evidence of interest in the training of teachers at the university level as early as

1831. The expression of that interest did not come to fruition until 1890 when the School of Pedagogy was established.

The years between saw growth and change in every facet of the national picture. Within the social framework there was change in population, both in size and character; there was change in the economy, in the nature and means of production and communication. On the educational scene there was stabilization of the common school, an awakened conscience regarding the quality of education, and a revolution in the theory and application of educational principles which changed the character of American education at every level. The era placed the stamp of progressivism on American education and cast teachers in almost impossible roles. They were expected to be artists of consumate skill, well grounded in their own fields, trained in the new science of pedagogy, and imbued with a zeal for social improvement. If they were to strive toward achieving these ideals, they needed help.

Heeding particularly the appeal of New York City's educational officials to provide the much needed pedagogical training for both teachers in service and prospective teachers, the School of Pedagogy offered instruction on the graduate level. Although the trend was toward placing scientific and professional education on this level, the variation in academic background of the students requesting admission to the School posed immediate administrative and instructional problems. Expedience dictated solutions to some of these and resulted in a split program requiring students to go outside of the units in which they wished to matriculate for part of their instruction. This was not an uncommon condition since the autonomy of the School of Pedagogy represented something of an historical accident. Such autonomy proved both a boon and a bane to these colleges. While it afforded some freedom to pioneer in pedagogical theory and practice, it led to an inexorable divorce from the arts and sciences that tore asunder the teacher-preparing function of the University and increasingly insulated the work of the pedagogical faculty.

Valiant efforts to match its program to the constantly shifting sands of social change produced a program characterized by innovation on the one hand but displaying reluctance to abandon established tradition on the other.

The range of interests of both faculty members and student body implied an institution geared toward meeting the needs for qualified teachers in a diversity of schools and classrooms.

The administration of the University of the City of New York demonstrated educational leadership in introducing the first teacher-training division on the graduate level as an integral part of a university structure. The officers and faculty of the School of Pedagogy gave evidence of leadership in opening up new areas of pedagogical instruction and in advancing the status of teaching. The beneficiaries of these opportunities came primarily from New York City and the metropolitan area.

A combination of circumstances developed by 1920 which impaired the effectiveness of the institution. Too local a student body, too great a dependence on a part-time faculty, limited finances and facilities, together with decreasing enrollments—all served to engender concern for the future of the teacher-preparing unit at New York University. But basic to these components were the cultural imperatives which had been gathering strength for more than a decade and which had reached the state of insistence following World War I. Again there were pressures which could not be ignored and demands which would not be denied. The educators at New York University recognized the need for change.

3 · The Need for Change

As the nineteenth century symbolized expansion, the twentieth century, from its outset, symbolized reform. No longer was the United States an insular entity. In economics, commerce, and politics, its activities extended beyond its borders, north, east, south, and west. As the country gained status as a world power, there was an accompanying awakening of the national conscience with regard to certain conditions at home. Responsibility for the under-privileged, recognition of the rights and needs of minority groups, and an obligation to eradicate corruption and vice in both business and politics on national and local levels were all concerns which culminated in the progressive movement, of which Theodore Roosevelt was a prime figure.

The extent of reform activity is visible on both the national and state levels. Within less than a decade, four amendments to the Constitution, commonly referred to as the progressive amendments, had been enacted.

The first of these, the sixteenth, predicted the expanding use of federal funds by authorizing Congress to impose taxes on incomes from whatever source derived, without apportionment among the states and without regard to any census or enumeration. Although the first proposal along these lines had been made as early as 1909, the amendment was ratified on February 25, 1913.

Within three months, on May 31, 1913, the Seventeenth Amendment providing for the popular election of United States senators indicated extension of the democratic principles of government.

A zealous effort in the direction of concern for the health and welfare of the nation came to fruition on January 29, 1919, with ratification of the Eighteenth Amendment imposing prohibition upon the land.

Finally, on August 26, 1920 women gained the franchise with the adoption of the Nineteenth Amendment granting women suffrage. This last reform had far-reaching implications for the status of women in various avenues of endeavor, including teaching.

By 1912, at the height of the progressive movement, there had been enacted in the states a considerable body of social legislation relating to wages and hours, the employment of women and children, and safety and health conditions in factories. In addition, under Theodore Roosevelt, forty-four antitrust suits had been started, and, under William Howard Taft, ninety proceedings against monopolies had been initiated.

The federal government become an active participant in education with the passage of two acts. The Smith-Lever Act of 1914 provided for a system of agricultural extension work based on cooperation between the Department of Agriculture and the land-grant colleges. Federal grants-in-aid were to be matched by state apporpriations in carrying out the program. The Smith-Hughes Act of 1917 provided for federal grants-in-aid, to be matched by the contributions of individual states, for promoting instruction in agriculture and the trades. It established a Federal Board for Vocational Education.

A review of the events—military, political, and business—engaging the United States in the first two decades of the twentieth century reveals activity extending from Mexico, on the nation's southwest border, to China and Japan, in the Far East, together with a number of incidents in the Caribbean and in Latin America.

Meanwhile, the Empire City was making its own bid for power and launching its own crusades for reform.

NEW YORK CITY BETWEEN 1900 AND 1920

In the early years of the twentieth century, New York City presented a paradoxical picture: beautiful and ugly, cosmopolitan and provincial, magnet to the ambitious, and Sodom to the preachers. The city enhanced its reputation by becoming the hub of creative America to which came the young and talented artists and writers from all the land. Most of these settled in the area surrounding New York University, at Washington Square in Greenwich Village.

With the coming of World War I, Harlem, at one time a pleasant suburb, became an overcrowded, complex part of the city. Job opportunities in New York led to mass migration from the South, and by 1920 more than 100,000 Negroes crowded into an area of approximately three square miles.

It was in this era that the lower East Side, long a blot

on the city's façade, lost—along with its color—much of its hopelessness through the work of the Russell Sage Foundation and through auxiliary services fostered by this organization. The foundation was an important agency of reform. Established in 1907 to improve social conditions throughout America, it encouraged and financed child and family welfare organizations in New York, aided in the development of social service workers and, in the 1920s, gave funds for the Committee on Regional Planning in New York City.

Evidence of a new respect for the common man was demonstrated in three ways: support for the establishment of the new free public library at Forty-Second Street and Fifth Avenue, keeping the Metropolitan Museum of Art open on Sundays so that the working man could enjoy its treasures on his one free day, and the development of mass-circulation journalism with newspapers ranging from the conservative to the sensational. The newspapers catered to the tastes of all segments of the city's teeming population.

THE CHANGING PEDAGOGICAL OUTLOOK

In countless cities and towns across the nation, educational innovations marked the years preceding World War I. Beginning with Dewey's Laboratory School in Chicago, educational experiments appeared in Menominee, Wisconsin; Fairhope, Alabama; Gary, Indiana; and Boston, Massachusetts. But once again New York City faced problems unique to itself and calling for pedagogical adjustments oriented to its own needs.

Sheer numbers, the constantly shifting population, and the variety of languages spoken in New York homes hampered educational progress. In addition, teachers themselves faced entirely new and unanticipated adjustments in these years of reform. They found themselves giving hundreds of baths each week, no mention of which appeared in any syllabi. By 1909, 74.1 percent of the children in New York City's schools were of foreign-born parentage, and the foreign-born group itself embraced some sixty distinct ethnic varieties.

The education of these youngsters called for more than surface change. Not only baths, but a great variety of other activities were begun. Manners, cleanliness, dress, and the business of getting along together had to be taught insistently and conscientiously. For the teacher this meant not only inculcating habits, attitudes, and values in the children, but often a complete reorientation of her own habits, attitudes, and values. To be multifaceted and adaptive were two essential attributes for the teacher during this period. Previous pedagogical instruction had made little, if any, reference to these extracurricular duties as part of any concept of teaching.

Finally, between the turn of the century and the first two decades of the twentieth century, several major trends affecting education in the United States may be said to have come to fruition. Each of these trends had its impetus in some development within the cultural milieu. Changing directions of education included:

1] universal acceptance of public secondary education,
2] establishment of the junior high school,

3] the rise of the progressive movement in education,

4] the increase in federal aid to education, with special reference to vocational education, and

5] the systematizing of the managerial aspects of education.

In the pages following, each of these trends will be discussed within its appropriate socio-cultural framework.

Universal Acceptance of Public Secondary Education
It has been stated that the outstanding achievement of the American school during the period from 1914 to 1928 was to make secondary education as universal as the previous hundred years had made primary education. The struggle to secure tax-supported post-elementary education was a fascinating one, for the free secondary school, embracing both college preparatory and terminal students, was a distinctive American creation.

The growing numbers of pupils continuing their education beyond the elementary level were attributable to several cultural factors. A major one was immigration which affected the schools in several ways. Not only were second-generation citizens swelling all school populations, but the elder generation had come to accept education as the instrument by which their offspring would achieve status and enhance their opportunities for ascent in the social and economic scale. Finding his voice through organized labor, the immigrant sought increased educational opportunities for his sons and daughters. Further, where formerly labor had opposed the expansion of education, it now encouraged it, for not only would a longer period of schooling be good for youth's enlightenment, it would serve to delay competition with the older group for steady employment. The urgent call for more secondary school teachers, as well as for teachers with more diversified skills, compelled teacher-training agencies to direct their attention to these demands. The trend toward universal secondary education was accompanied by the following significant movement within the field itself.

Establishment of the Junior High School

In the search to make the educational experiences of youth more meaningful in terms of the growing complexity of American life, educators began to evaluate the advantages of reorganizing the educational system. The pressure for some change in the eight-year elementary, four-year secondary organization appeared as early as the 1880s.

In an address at a New Orleans meeting of the National Education Association, J. E. Seaman drew a relationship between the high school and the increasing demands of American industrial life. Such an institution, he maintained, had to stand as a friend of the laboring man who would more and more regard this rung on the educational ladder as the leveler of the distinction between rich and poor as far as power and place were concerned. But, said Seaman, this would be so ". . . only if the high school continued to modify its program in terms of the needs of the times."

Three years later, before a meeting of the Department of Superintendence of the National Educational

Association, President Charles W. Eliot called attention to an overcrowded secondary program succeeding a rather narrow elementary curriculum and noted the effect of this situation on the ages and background of entering freshmen in college. A further issue at this level was the need to provide a more functional program for those students who did not plan to go to college. Discussions such as these stimulated the appointment of several National Educational Association committees which directed their attention to these problems. One of these groups, the Committee of Ten, was concerned with the reorganization of secondary education. Finding it impossible to effect improvement within the existing educational system, this group recommended either assigning some of the secondary school subjects to the elementary school or extending the secondary period down two years, leaving six for the elementary curriculum. Response to such pressure for change came in the form of the junior high school. Between 1910 and 1918, 557 junior high schools with more than 116,000 students, were established in the United States. One effect of this organization was to permit expansion of industrial, trade, and vocational curricula in the senior high school, thus making it a more practical experience for the terminal students.

The Rise of the Progressive Movement in Education
Pedagogical protest during the 1870s and 1880s had been local, intermittent, and frequently innocuous. By contrast, the 1890s brought a nationwide torrent of criticism, innovation, and reform that soon took on all the earmarks of a social movement. The articles of

Joseph Mayer Rice appearing in the *Forum* were the first to weave the many strands of contemporary protest into a single reform program.

Once under way, the reform movement manifested itself in a remarkable diversity of pedagogical protest and innovation. From its beginning it was pluralistic, often self-contradictory, and always closely related to broader currents of social and political progressivism.

Meyer points out that the founding of the Progressive Education Association in 1919 gave a vigorous organizational voice to what formerly had been a loosely-joined revolt against pedagogical formalism.

The progressive education movement enlisted parents and teachers, starry-eyed crusaders, and hard-headed politicians. While there were schisms among progressives when they formed their association in 1919, they had established some commonly-accepted propositions. Following is a digest of these propositions as given by Meyer:

1] that school should be "child-centered" and that the child should be permitted to develop along the lines of his natural bents and interests;

2] that learning should take place at a pace which is never forced;

3] that learning should come from active experience rather than from memorized facts or rote learning;

4] that education should be concerned not only with the intellectual, but with the civic, and the mental, physical, and emotional welfare of the individual; and

5] that the home and the school, aided by science, must labor hand in hand to accomplish the desired result.

Progressivism in education demanded new techniques of instruction from the kindergarten through the university. In less than two generations it transformed the character of the American school. The teacher education agency which failed in some measure to harken to the demands of its precepts stood in danger of being considered out-of-step and thereby of facing curtailed enrollments.

The Increase in Federal Aid to Education with special reference to Vocational Education

Although industrial education may be said to have been touched off by the Della Vos methods exhibited at the Philadelphia Centennial Exposition of 1876, the year 1910 marks a turning point in the vocational education movement for a number of reasons. A survey in that year revealed that twenty-nine states had provided for some form of industrial education; of these, ten had provided for technical high schools, eighteen for manual training, eleven for domestic science, nineteen for agricultural training, and eleven for industrial and trade courses. Despite the fact that the movement, calling for large expenditures and involving sweeping changes in curriculum and method, had received prompt legislative recognition in at least twenty-five states, leaders began to display the impatience characteristic of reformers. They began to dream of by-passing an arduous state-by-state campaign with a massive bid for federal assistance.

The story of the campaign that began in 1910 with the defeated Dolliver Bill and culminated in 1917 with the passage of the Smith-Hughes Act providing federal aid for secondary vocational education is an exciting chapter in the politics of American education. The challenge to education was to keep its teachers and its facilities abreast of the onrush of technological advance.

The Systematizing of the Managerial Aspects of Education

As education became "big business" following the Civil War, it engendered a prodigious growth in the techniques and agencies of school administration. Nowhere was this better illustrated than in the existence of 27,000 administrative and supervisory officers as reported by the end of World War I. The power of the state in education, by this time, was embodied in the state superintendency and the state board of education. Large city school systems followed a similar organization pattern, with powers delegated by the legislature to a board of education and a city superintendent as the chief local school officer. Administrative relationships changed. As schools and school systems became larger, bureaucracy increased. School administration became a separate professional function rather than a supplementary responsibility of the senior teachers.

Although certification practices are characterized by heterogeneity in the United States, great impetus to the improvement of qualifications of new teachers, together with the upgrading of teachers in service, came with centralization of the licensing function in the several state departments of education. The institution of more stringent licensing requirements was accompanied by certain reform measures in teacher training agencies which (1) raised the requirements for admission to normal schools to include high school graduation, (2) extended the length of the normal school course by two years to give more time for cultural subjects and the mastery of subject matter, and (3) widened the scope of the offerings to care for the preparation of secondary school teachers.

During the early decades of the twentieth century, additional centralizing trends helped to improve the professional status of the teacher. These represented adjuncts of the licensing provisions and included:

1] the substitution of approved training for teachers' examinations,

2] the differentiation of certificates according to the nature of the student's preparation and the abandonment of blanket licenses,

3] the gradual abolition of life certificates,

4] the raising of training levels for all types of teaching certificates, with some inclination to make four years of training above high school graduation the minimum for teaching in the elementary school and five years the minimum for the secondary school, and

5] the requirement of a certain number of specialized courses in education in the candidate's program of studies.

Closely allied to these social and educational developments was the increasing role which women played both in their formulation and in their implementation. Spurred by the political freedom granted them by enactment of the Nineteenth Amendment, women no longer viewed their sex as a hindrance to more active participation in the educational reforms of the times. Feminine educators such as Patty Smith Hill found new converts for the experiments they were conducting in a variety of situations.

Margaret Naumburg in the Children's School (later the Walden School) and Caroline Pratt in the Play School (later the City and Country School) each sought to apply pedagogical theories advanced by the Progressive Education Association. In 1921 the Beaver Country Day School was founded by two ladies who had come upon John and Evelyn Dewey's *Schools of Tomorrow* and liked what they read.

The establishment of Lincoln School at Teachers College, Columbia University in 1916 brought together an unusually imaginative faculty including Nell Curtis, Martha Groggel, Lula Wright, and Satis Coleman. These women, in addition to possessing a new freedom in classroom techniques, cooperated in producing curriculum guides, texts, workbooks, teaching units, and achievement tests—activities sparsely entered into by women a quarter of a century earlier. The opportunity for expressing their own personal individualities in the exercise of their profession brought a new relationship between teacher and pupil. The seed was sown for recognition of human relations as an integral part of the educative process.

THE STATUS OF EDUCATION IN NEW YORK CITY
IN THE INTERBELLUM ERA

New York City, centered as it was in much of the changing pedagogical mainstream, did not manifest in its own public education system the same eagerness to adopt the pedagogical innovations which were being tried out in a number of private institutions throughout the country.

Between 1901–05 attempts were made to introduce the arts as a unit of study, shop work, and nature study including school gardens. But in 1904 the city comptroller charged the school superintendent with extravagance. He claimed that a large saving could be effected by discontinuing special subjects. In addition, this would afford teachers and pupils more time to concentrate on the "three Rs." The subjects he attacked were drawing, manual training, sewing, cooking, music, physical training, nature study, and foreign languages. A questionnaire to parents showed overwhelming support for continuing such studies, and after a year of debate it was decided that the subjects should be retained.

Although these advances may be looked upon as indications of things to come, essentially the decade 1900–10 was still one in which most educators adhered to a concept of child development in which stress was placed upon discipline and restraint, upon rote learning, repetition, and upon passive rather than active learning.

In 1913 the Common School Inquiry, sometimes referred to as the Hanus Survey, found that in the elementary schools both the teaching and the subject matter were too formalized. The committee recommended greater individualization and flexibility for better adaptation to practical problems of contemporary life. The committee further recommended creation of a bureau for research and curriculum development, the hiring of adequate clerical staffs to free principals and supervisors for professional work, and the simplification of the administrative machinery of the system.

New York City experimented with the Gary Plan during 1914–15 but did not find it successful in the light of existing facilities and schedules. This plan had been evolved by William Wirt when he was superintendent of schools at Gary, Indiana. The essence of the scheme was to balance the instructional program between curricular divisions, looking toward the most efficient use of the school plant. By organizing students into two groups, with the groups changing rooms once in the morning and once in the afternoon, such specialized facilities as the gymnasium, shops, home economics rooms, music and art rooms, science laboratories, and assembly halls could be utilized with maximum efficiency and the school could be made to reflect an embryonic community life. The initial intention was to keep the school open all day, twelve months a year, and to all age groups.

The most consistent advances during the decade 1900–10 were made in the area of school administration. As early as 1900, the superintendent reported that it would never be possible to bring the city school system to the standard of efficiency which it ought to attain until the responsibility for every weakness in the schools could be directly located and until the administrative machinery was simplified. To this end, he advocated that full authority for all matters affecting the schools be placed in the city board of education. On February 3, 1902 the education section of the revised city charter became effective. The most important changes were the centralization of power in the hands of the board of education, acting through properly constituted executive departments.

By 1910 there were 800 kindergarten, vacation, and evening school teachers, and another 18,000 teachers were employed by the board of education in the day schools alone. Between 1917 and 1920 a series of events occurred which markedly improved the lot of New York City teachers. Among these were establishment of the retirement board, rescinding of the law against employment of married teachers, and victory for women teachers in their fight for salaries equal to those paid to men.

There was more turmoil surrounding the schools during the decade 1910–20 than in any since the city was consolidated. During these years, as educators became more dissastified with the accomplishments of the schools, new ideas began to take root. Improved practices in scattered schools by forward-looking teachers and supervisors proved to be the harbingers of the fundamental changes of the next decade.

THE SCHOOL OF PEDAGOGY ON THE EVE OF WORLD WAR I

While the School of Pedagogy of New York University demonstrated an intent to reflect the changing social order by introducing courses allied to these interests, such as the preparation of teachers for work with the handicapped, methods courses for such special subjects as art, music, and foreign languages, and instruction in commercial subjects, there is less evidence of attention to the important studies in child development which were leading to an entirely new concept of classroom procedures. The field of sociology did not show signs of growth in the School of Pedagogy during these years of major social reforms. There was continued emphasis on the psychological theories of behavior and learning but few illustrations of their application in the teaching situation. Manual training again was largely confined to its uses with the backward and defective child.

It would appear that the program failed to achieve the

desired balance between the arts and the sciences which educational leaders were urging and for which public education was striving. In this sense, it is conceivable that the School of Pedagogy was not preparing teachers in sufficient range or depth to equip them for the more creative approaches to teaching demanded by the new education.

In the field of administration, too, while this subject had been mentioned among the offerings of the School of Pedagogy from the beginning, titles and descriptions of courses in this area remain practically unchanged during the thirty-year period of the School's existence.

It is apparent from various statements that Dean Balliet was not entirely unaware of the state of affairs. There was reference to the need for strengthening the secondary education department and adding an expanded and improved program in administration. Even at this point, however, no direct mention was made of the impact of progressivism on either the culture or education.

Despite the evidence of its pioneering spirit, the School of Pedagogy had not been successful in overcoming its two persistent weaknesses: limited funds, and inadequate staff and facilities. With the continued decrease in enrollment it was not likely that much progress could be hoped for in either of these directions.

SUMMARY

Although many changes in the cultural and educational scene were in the making well before World War I, that event makes a great divide in the history of American society.

Freud had delivered his first lecture in this country in

1909. *Poetry,* the magazine which gave many talented young men and women their first chance to publish, was founded in 1912. The year 1913 saw modern art introduced to over 100,000 New Yorkers in the now famous Armory Show, and 1914–15 witnessed the emergence of two brilliant writers—one journalistic and one literary—Walter Lippmann and Van Wyck Brooks respectively. Culturally, America was coming of age.

Early in the century, spearheaded by the advent of Theodore Roosevelt to the presidency, sources of corruption in public and private enterprises were vigorously routed. A wave of settlement houses, together with hundreds of trained social workers, attested to the growing social conscience.

Each of these developments in its own way symbolized a break with the past, a revolt not only against the dearly-held traditions of the conservatists but against the moralizing of progressives as well. Progressivisim was on the march, and no component in the complex organism of the expanding democracy wholly escaped its influence.

The country at large responded with legislation which affected the welfare of its citizens from the most isolated farmhouse to the most crowded tenement. The extension of educational opportunity, the improvement of living standards, recognition that effective education required effective management, and the great forward movements toward vitalizing the curriculum at every level were part of the heritage of this interbellum era.

There could be no doubt that education would be affected. With the "melting pot" reproduced in every urban classroom, teachers faced new challenges and new tasks. With the educative process increasingly tied in with that of the social, reorganization of structure and function was the order of the day in the classroom and in the community.

While many of the ideas and practices of progressive education germinated in New York City, the impact of reform was national in scope. However, as a prophet is not without honor save in his own country, so many of the pedagogical innovations were tried in small private schools throughout the nation before they were accorded recognition in the public school system of New York City. So, too, there was an apparent lag in developing a new blueprint for teacher education in the School of Pedagogy of New York University. Dean Balliet pointed out the need for the School to cover a larger part of the field of education. In his 1917–18 annual report he stated: "The policy of the school is, at present, to do strong work in a limited field, but this field is at present too limited to make a strong appeal to advanced students."

In recommending expansion of the program, Balliet pointed out the need for increasing the faculty, including, he maintained, ". . . men who are not merely scholars, but men who also are skillful teachers and exemplify good teaching in their own classes; and above all, men who have had practical experience as teachers in high schools, as principals, or superintendents of schools."

With foresight, however, Balliet did call attention to the need for more publicity both for the School of Pedagogy and for the University as a whole. He recommended that members of the faculty should represent the School, at the University's expense, at annual meetings of the

National Education Association, the superintendents' convention, and the American Association for the Advancement of Science which had a section on education.

The dean further urged the establishment of an undergraduate department, the conferring of a bachelor's degree in education, and the transfer of all courses to which education credit was given in the Washington Square College to the School of Pedagogy, and the granting of the master of arts and doctor of philosophy degrees in the School of Pedagogy as well as in the Graduate School.

Notwithstanding these progressive recommendations, Jones[1] reported that the situation, both internally in terms of faculty morale and externally in terms of diminishing enrollments, had shown steady deterioration. As a consequence, by 1920 the University authorities were forced to recognize that the need for change was imperative if the institution was to continue to meet its obligation to society in the important area of teacher education.

With the approval of the University Council, the Chancellor of the University, Dr. Elmer Ellsworth Brown, offered the deanship of the School of Pedagogy to Dr. John W. Withers, then superintendent of schools at St. Louis, Missouri. There followed an exchange of letters between Chancellor Brown and Dr. Withers. Excerpts from these communications may throw some light on the seriousness with which the Council members and the Chancellor viewed the matter of selecting a dean for the School of Pedagogy and the prevailing financial status of administrative officers in the University:

[1] Theodore F. Jones, New York University, 1832–1932.

I. Letter from Elmer E. Brown to John W. Withers, January 9, 1920:

I am very glad there is some likelihood that you may be able to come to us for a lecture some time before the close of this month. The meeting which you are to address is to be given by itself, and not as a part of a series. The audience will be made up generally of instructors and advanced students in the University, together with graduates of our School of Pedagogy and others engaged in the supervision and teaching of schools in the metropolitan area.

The purpose of the meeting is to give this company of educators an opportunity of hearing your views on the educational problems pressing for solution, in the belief that you can contribute something that will be of value to the teaching world in a time of so great educational stress and strain.

II. Letter from John W. Withers to Elmer E. Brown, February 11, 1920:

. . . I feel that your Council Committee, acting no doubt on your recommendation, have been exceedingly generous in the offer they have made. I cannot consciously (sic) ask you to pay mare than $8000, if other Deans, who are able men and who have been with you for some time, must continue to receive much smaller remunerations. I am convinced, however, that the University cannot hope to keep men of high ability in these positions, men who have the ability you need to build up the University in accordance with the plans you have in mind, without a considerable increase over present salaries. . . .

It may be of some interest to indicate a reaction of an officer of a neighboring teacher-training institution to the possibility that Dr. Withers would come to New York University.

On March 26, 1920 Dr. Paul Monroe, director of the

School of Education of Teachers College, Columbia University, wrote to Dr. Withers:

III.

Some time ago I had the pleasure of suggesting to Chancellor Brown of the New York University, that you were the man best fitted in the whole country to take the deanship of their School of Education. He writes me that he has since offered you this place and I am writing to tell you that we should be greatly pleased at Teachers College to have you in our community and to have a man of your standing and ability with whom we might cooperate in our common work.

The New York University in its School of Education (sic) has always had close affiliations with the city school system—closer than we have here at Columbia; but there are other features and purposes which made this place attractive, and while of course it is not Teachers College, we are willing to admit that there are others. I should be greatly interested in having the opportunity of cooperating with you and commend New York and this position to your earnest consideration.

Again, on March 29, 1920 Calvin N. Kendall, commissioner of education for the state of New Jersey, wrote to Withers:

IV.

. . . Point number two is that I am interested for the sake of the schools in New Jersey that they get a good man at the head of their department of education at New York University, because a great many of our New Jersey teachers take courses there and the character of their department, therefore, is of great interest to us.

Finally, Dr. John H. Finley, president of the University of the State of New York, state education department at Albany, New York wrote to Dr. Withers:

V.

Chancellor Brown has just told me in confidence of his proffer to you. I give it most cordial support because I am wishing that we could have you within reach here in New York. It would be a great help to us. . . .

Before making a final decision, Dr. Withers requested the opportunity to make a survey of the state of educational affairs with the following objectives:

1] to analyze the prevailing conditions with respect to the School of Pedagogy,

2] to evaluate the relation of the School of Pedagogy to other teacher-training institutions in New York City, and

3] to determine the role and function of such a school if it could be demonstrated that there was a place for it at New York University and a need for it in the metropolitan New York area.[2]

The results of this survey convinced Withers that there was a place and a need for such a school, and in September 1920 he accepted the offer and was appointed dean of the School of Pedagogy. Shortly thereafter, he presented to the chancellor and the members of the University council a plan for reorganization of the School which, after due consideration, was approved in its entirety. With the approval of these recommendations, the first one of which called for a change in the name of the division from the School of Pedagogy to the School of Education, there was launched a new and broader concept of the obligation of the professional school in preparing men and women for educational service in many roles.

[2] Correspondence and other materials were made available to the writer by Dean Withers at Bradenton, Florida in September, 1955.

Part II
Through the First Fifty Years

4 · The School of Education in the Formative Years 1921–1928

Following the liberating influences of the first world war generally and the Nineteenth Amendment specifically, women teachers were given, not only equal pay with male teachers, but a larger voice in the building of their profession. Gradually both recognition and status were acquired.

With greater responsibility to curriculum-making came greater assurance in meeting pupil needs and a sense of growing professional competence. This latter was further strengthened by wider participation in education organizations and national conventions and by sharing experiences through the growing body of educational publications. Out of such contacts came a stronger sense of professional unity.

The sounds of change in the world around them were heard as a clarion call within many institutions devoted to teacher preparation to champion the new in the evolving profession. Not only did such institutions face the challenge of bringing their own educational philosophies and programs into line with contemporary thought, but they were under the necessity of recognizing that the framework within which they operated had to be extended to embrace the entire realm of educational endeavor.

When on May 27, 1921 the Council of New York University authorized the change in name of the teacher-education division from the School of Pedagogy to the School of Education, they wittingly—or perhaps unwittingly—made it possible for Dean Withers to recommend further changes intended to bring the School of Education into the forefront of such institutions.

PROPOSED CHANGES

Immediately upon assuming the deanship, Withers submitted a series of recommendations for reorganizing the division in such a way that it would symbolize the prevailing broader and more comprehensive concept of the role of a professional school such as this one. The suggested plans contemplated four major changes:

1] change in the designation of its degrees from master and doctor of pedagogy to master of arts and doctor of philosophy,

2] establishment of programs for the preparation of men and women for administrative and supervisory posts in the educational system,

3] encouragement of research through the use of local schools as laboratories for survey purposes and for the solution of educational problems (This activity was viewed as rendering a service to education at the same time.), and

4] stimulation of increased enrollment by an appeal to a wider segment of the population.

The Council's approval of the recommendations left the

dean free to begin the complicated task of reconstructing the School.

REVISED AIMS AND PURPOSES

The objectives implicit in the four contemplated changes provided the basis for the School's restated aims and purposes. These appeared in the annual bulletins of the School of Education from 1921 through 1938, the full period of Withers' administration. The substance of these modified aims is contained in the opening statement which read: "The purpose of the School of Education is the preparation of men and women for educational service, both locally and in the wider field of American education."

In commenting upon the tasks of reorganization, the dean emphasized that the institution would place major emphasis upon the improvement of educational practice and secondary emphasis upon the improvement of theory.

Withers further recommended to the faculty that in the plan for broadening its sphere of influence, the School of Education should seek an effective articulation with other education agencies in order to:

1] render more available the resources of the School of Education for service to the state and the city,

2] open the way to experimental study of teacher training on a large scale,

3] open the way for a broader and clearer understanding of the place and function of the School of Education among these agencies and in the whole field of educational service, and

4] exemplify by demonstration what sort of articulation between such an institution as the School of Education and the legally constituted agencies for the training of teachers in a state would be of most service and mutually most stimulating to this high endeavor.

The document went on to suggest a plan for the achievement of these ends and recommended, among other things, establishment of a junior teachers college to serve as a laboratory school and to provide a resource for experimentation and research. However, for budgetary and other reasons this suggestion was never implemented.

If the administration and the faculty of the School of Education were to accomplish the stated objectives, several basic issues had to be resolved, among which was the reorganization of the unit itself. This had to be of such nature and scope that the School could include the breadth of course offerings essential to the fulfillment of its newly conceived mission and that it could adequately serve both pre-service and in-service applicants. One of the first steps, therefore, was to secure approval from the University Council to incorporate an undergraduate as well as a graduate division. Authorization for this step was secured in January, 1924, and the purposes of the two divisions were announced in the bulletin for 1924–25. For the undergraduate division two points were stressed: provision for teachers-in-service to earn a bachelor's degree without interrupting their careers, and opportunity to discover qualified students who should be encouraged to continue their professional education in the graduate division. The purposes of the graduate division were expressed in a larger context of providing leadership in American education and of developing a philosophy of education and educational policy suited to the increasingly complex needs of American life.

A second step essential to moving the institution toward the accomplishment of its objectives was to expand and enrich the program of the School of Education by the addition of staff and course offerings. Between 1922 and 1924 the dean requested authorization to establish thirteen professorships and urged that these positions be filled by the best available persons the University could secure. Within three years these appointments had been made, along with ten instructors, fourteen assistant professors, and five associate professor ranks.

With the purposes and objectives of the teacher-education center fairly well established, the next imperative was to develop an internal structure and administrative machinery which would insure efficient functioning of the organization.

ADMINISTRATIVE INNOVATIONS

During the first two decades of the twentieth century there were only sporadic evidences on the national scene of concern with making administration more democratic. It would be another twenty years before principles governing democratic action would be enunciated. Then, such principles would include the following:

1] facilitating the continuous growth of individual and social personalities by providing all persons with opportunities to participate actively in all enterprises that concern them,
2] recognizing that leadership is a function of every individual, and to encourage the exercise of leadership by each person in accordance with his interests, needs, and abilities,

3] providing means by which persons could plan together, share their experiences, and cooperatively evaluate their achievements, and

4] placing the responsibility for making decisions that affect the total enterprise with the group rather than with one or a few individuals.[1]

What follows, therefore, would suggest that the administrative officers and the faculty of the School of Education gave evidence of being in the forefront with regard to this development in the academic milieu.

In 1925, the dean appointed a committee of the faculty to prepare and submit for faculty approval a faculty-administration organization for the efficient operation of the School's affairs. The Committee on Committees, as this body was called, submitted its report to the faculty on October 20, 1925, and prefaced its recommendations with the following statements:

It is only fair to those who have worked out these proposals and to those to whom they are submitted for study and possible approval, that we should set forth the cardinal principles of cooperation underlying the form of organization here proposed. In brief they are these:

(1) That the more fully the members of this Faculty share responsibility with the Dean in the formulation of the distinctive educational policies of 'our' School of Education, the more intelligently, whole-heartedly, and effectively, will they be able to work for the complete and early realization of our distinctive institutional objectives.

(2) That the more widely the responsibility for administrative services is distributed in the ranks of the teaching corps, the greater the likelihood that there will develop a common understanding of the complexity of our administrative problems and along with that understanding an increased

[1] G. Robert Koopmen, Alice Miel, and Paul J. Misner, *Democracy in School Administration*, pp. 3–5.

desire to do our best, each in his own place and in his own way, to reduce waste effort and to prevent the friction that renders the best teaching impossible.

(3) That it is obviously unfair to require, or even to allow the Dean or other administrative officers to bear an unreasonable burden of labor, and

(4) That consistent efforts should be made to free the Dean from every demand that would tend to delay his progress in carrying out the major plans he is making for further institutional development.

The committee proposed the establishment of eight standing committees to formulate educational policies and to set up general administrative procedures. The eight committees were as follows:

I. Committee on Admissions and Student Standing—Undergraduate Division

II. Committee on Admissions and Student Standing—Graduate Division

III. Committee on Educational Placement and Service

IV. Committee on Faculty-Student-Alumni Relationships

V. Committee on Publications and Publicity

VI. Committee on Curricula (sic) Adjustment and Revision

VII. Committee on Intra- and Inter-School Scholarships

VIII. Committee on Building Plans

There was to be, in addition, a General Committee, with assigned functions as indicated below:

1] Counsel with the Dean in the determination of functions to be assigned by him to each of the several Standing Committees.

2] Cooperate with the Dean in the supervision and coordination of the work of the several Standing Committees and in the preparation of programs for regular and special meetings of the General Faculty and of the Major Faculty.

3] Recommend:

a] The discontinuance of any Standing Committees thought to be no longer needed.

b] The formation of new or additional committees thought to be needed.

4] Devise ways and means for promoting the effective cooperation and, when feasible, the active participation of students with the several committees of the Major Faculty.

5] Serve as a clearing house for all researches undertaken by members of the Faculty or by students, on the problems of the several Standing Committees.

6] Serve as an Advisory Council to the Dean:

a] in the preparation of the calendar of public events,

b] in the conduct of major conferences with the field forces in public education, and

c] in any other matters in which counsel is requested by him.

The proposal further recommended that:

The Dean or the Acting Dean serve as Chairman of the General Committee and name the Chairman of each of the several Standing Committees to serve during his pleasure.

The Dean or the Acting Dean appoint each member of the Major Faculty to at least one of the eight Standing Committees and that these appointments shall be for the period of one year.

Lest the reader assume that the general committee was set up to check the power of the dean, the following paragraph from the report of the Committee on Committees is offered:

The suggestion that the present organization of our faculty is inadequate to meet the demands for a satisfactory formulation of our Educational policies or for the effective administration of a rapidly expanding program carries with it no implied criticism of any one—least of all of the Dean whose accomplishments have been as prodigious as his tasks have been Herculean in the period of the recent unprecedented expansion of our institutional program and service.

The rationale for the proposals made rests on several factors, among which were the unprecedented growth of the school and the rapid expansion of the scope of institutional service; both of these tended to render obsolete an organization conceived and planned to meet "the situation as it existed but yesterday."

The fulfillment of the recommendations in this report created an administrative-faculty structure which did not basically change in the years between its original adoption and the terminal year of this study.

Further expansion in the organizational design of the School took place during the year 1926–27 when the administration of the institution was enlarged to include two assistant deans, E. George Payne to handle matters of instruction and Milton E. Loomis to manage financial affairs. Thus, by the end of the academic year 1928–29, a structural plan for the School of Education had emerged which contained essential elements of democratic administration and the provision for internal mobility which assured, as far as possible, total participation of the faculty in the establishment of policy and the conduct of academic affairs.

RESUMÉ

As late as the mid-thirties, the achievement of democratic administration in education remained as one of the factors hindering educational progress. Autocratic administration still was responsible for curbing much initiative and stamping out originality among teachers. It is all the more unique, therefore, to find the staff of the professional School of Education adopting in 1925 a scheme of administration as democratically oriented as that proposed by the Committee on Committees, imperfect though it may have been. Such imperfection may be ascribed to the fact that the dean was to serve as chairman of the General Committee, from which major policy would emerge; the dean was to name the chairman of each of the standing committees; and the dean was to assign each member of the faculty to one of the committees with no indication of a provision for the exercise of choice on the part of the faculty member. However, it must be noted that the Committee on Committees reserved for the faculty ultimate decision in policy-making, since recommendations of the General Committee or of any one of the standing committees had to be ratified by the entire faculty before they could become effective.

The recency of appointment of most members of the major faculty, with the attendant lack of familiarity with the School's problems as well as unfamiliarity with each other, may have led to a condition under which initial recommendations had, perforce, to reflect the stamp of an individual personality. To some extent, therefore, and because of necessity, the leadership in the first four or five years of the School's existence was of the front-line variety with lines of action proposed largely by one individual, Dean Withers.

With the structure designed and in operation, the teacher-education division at New York University was now ready to attempt to carry out its stated aims through an enriched and on-going program.

THE PROGRAM

Referring to the reconstituted pedagogical unit at New York University, Chancellor Elmer E. Brown noted that, both in New York City and throughout the land, the time was ripe for a major forward movement in public education, one in which the School of Education could be expected to take a leading part.

With increasing recognition of the inadequacies of existing teacher-training programs came a growing national awareness of the limitations of teachers whose cultural backgrounds were bounded by three or four elementary school disciplines, and whose professional preparation was as meager as that provided in the short course of the normal schools.

The primary instrument by which the School of Education could demonstrate its response to the various cultural issues pressing for attention was a revitalized and expanded program. In the transition from the School of Pedagogy to the School of Education, some departments remained relatively unchanged in terms of course listings. Such departments included experimental education and philosophy and history of education. This situation may have been somewhat related to the dean's earlier statement of intention to place less emphasis on the improvement of theory than on the improvement of practice in education. In all other areas of instruction, the program showed modification and expansion. In psychology, the School of Pedagogy had listed courses which dealt in a large part with the findings of the scientific movement which reached its peak in the nineteenth century. In 1923 the name of this department was changed to educational psychology. Thereafter, the offerings were increased and the application of these findings to the learning process became the central core of study in this discipline.

To assess the degree to which the program in the School of Education of New York University met the contemporary challenges, the specific issues of the 1920s referred to in Chapter III, are here recapitulated and an attempt made to indicate the ways by which course offerings in individual departments contributed toward these ends.

Universal Acceptance of Public Secondary Education
Establishment of the Junior High School

More than twenty years after President Eliot's first urgings for reorganization of the educational system, several cities became aware of the growing indictment of the "8-4-4" plan as a means of discharging the added obligations which social change was placing upon the schools. By 1917, 272 towns claimed to have junior high schools, but by 1922, eleven percent of all public high schools were classified as reorganized schools; that is, as junior high, junior-senior and undivided, and senior high schools.

Beyond the need for additional teachers to staff the secondary schools as greater percentages of the population continued into the high schools, there was a continuing demand in both the junior and senior high schools for teachers in an increased number of specializations. This demand was augmented by the greatly expanded secondary school curricula. Teachers were needed for such special subjects as trades, agriculture, home economics, physical education, and the arts.

In addition, with more variation and flexibility in the groupings of students and especially as schools became larger, guidance programs were developed in an effort to take account of these varying needs and concerns of pupils. This created a demand for trained personnel to fill these extracurricular posts.

An examination of the program in the School of Education between 1921 and 1928 reveals courses dealing with the organization and administration of both the junior and senior high school. The changing curricula in these institutions, influenced by the progressive movement, were studied, and attention was given to the problems attendant upon such reorganization. Instruction was offered on the new role of the teacher as an adviser, and methods courses were taught for every subject from algebra to typewriting. Mathematics, the sciences, languages, the social studies, the language arts, and commerical subjects were areas included in these courses. The theory, principles, practices, and problems of part-time and continuing education, industrial, technical, and vocational education also were scrutinized through the work of this department. Work in supervision and in tests and measurements adapted to this level constituted a part of this department's considerations, and observation and practice teaching were provided for the potential secondary school teacher.

Beginning in 1921 with sixteen courses, fourteen of which were methods courses, the offerings of this department more than doubled by 1924 and reached a total of forty-four by 1926.

It would appear that little relating to the structure, operation, theory, and curriculum of secondary level institutions was overlooked in the work of the Department of Secondary Education between 1921 and 1928.

The Rise of the Progressive Movement in Education

During the early decades of the twentieth century there was proclaimed an educational discovery of far-reaching implications, namely, that the creative impulse is within the child himself. The implications of this postulate had a twofold significance: first, that every child is born with the power to create, and second, that it is the task of the school to provide an environment which will draw out this creative power.

In 1925 the School of Education made its initial gesture in this direction by introducing such courses as *Creative Aspects of Contemporary Life, The Creative Impulse, Creative Reading,* and *Experiments in Creative Education.* A Department of Creative Education was established in 1928.

The Department of Secondary Education responded to

the influence of this movement with such courses as *The Activity Program* and *Creative High School Control.*

Interest in this tenet of progressivism at the elementary level was manifested through such listings as *The Creative Impulse in Children and Adults* and *Creative Reading.* Following 1928 these courses were transferred from the Department of Elementary Education to the Department of Creative Education.

Throughout the early years of the institution, the work of the Department of Elementary Education had pointed to awareness on the part of the faculty that the time had passed for viewing elementary education as concerned primarily with the three Rs. Continuing the policy first noted in the School of Pedagogy, the department addressed itself to preparing teachers for the mentally retarded, the blind, and other types of handicapped children such as those with special speech defects. The developing field of supervision was not neglected, and in line with the liberalizing concepts of early childhood teaching fostered by the progressive education movement, there was a course entitled *The Teaching of Nature Study.*

Another indication of sensitivity to the contemporary scene was the inclusion of work in the language arts at the elementary level, such studies having continued to gain prominence following an investigation by President Eliot, of Harvard, which revealed the very limited acquaintance which children in the elementary schools had with these areas. Attention was given to administrative, curricular, and instructional problems relating to this level, and again there was an opportunity for observation and practice teaching. Within these seven years, however, the only work relating to the teaching of children in kindergarten or nursery school was one course in *Stories and Story Telling* which, by the description of the course, adapted such materials and techniques to this age level. This would appear to be a notable lack on the part of the staff and the dean in the Department of Elementary Education in the light of the fact that, in the years following World War I, kindergarten and nursery schools flourished as the number of working women rose.

THE INFLUENCE OF SOCIAL CHANGE ON THE PROGRAM

As technology influenced such areas as the national economy, business, industry, and education, there arose a need for a social technology. The shift from a reliance on laissez-faire, with its faith in automatic adjustment, to a reliance on social design, created a vastly different world for youth and a new center of interest for education. The problems of the nation and the community had been relatively simple while the United States remained essentially rural. With the transformation of the country into a great industrial domain, the problems of social policy became increasingly complex. One of the most important obligations of the school, therefore, became the preparation of youth to grapple with fundamental issues woven into the whole fabric of social relationships.

The relatively extensive work in educational sociology immediately introduced into the teacher-education program gave evidence of the sensitivity on the part of the leadership of the School of Education to this obligation.

From its second year of operation onward, the School

of Education trained teachers and workers in social and community agencies and in the sociological bases of behavior. Components of the social milieu which came under investigation included immigrant and citizenship education, poverty, social welfare, accident prevention, and juvenile delinquency. In the catalogues' alphabetical range, from adult to vocational education, the implications of the influence of the environment were probed in terms of personality and social adjustment and from the view of education as social control.

The range of these offerings suggests that, perhaps in this field, the School of Education responded not only to cultural demands, but led the way in bringing discussions of such topics as social pathology and education, the nature and needs of the child in social life, the problem child in school, and the sociological determination of the curriculum into the program of professional education.

Of the work of this department, Withers wrote:

There are three distinct lines along which the Department of Educational Sociology is working and in which it hopes to make distinct contributions: first, a contribution to teaching; second, its contribution to education, and third, its contribution to research. The work of teaching will always remain one of the most important functions of the department and in this aspect there has been notable development. . . . The department, during the past year, has originated and published the first volume of the Journal of Educational Sociology. It is the first journal in this field, and, therefore has done pioneer work in emphasizing the place of sociology in education.

In the third field . . . this has been the most fruitful year in the history of the department. An elaborate research project, unique of its kind, is to be carried out utilizing the Boys'

Club recently established in New York City as the laboratory for the investigation.[2]

Increased Federal Aid to Education with Particular Reference to Vocational Education

Federal aid for vocational education resulted in part from changes wrought by unprecedented advances in technology. These changes had rendered obsolete previous methods such as apprenticeship and on-the-job training for gainful occupation. These developments led to personnel and curriculum problems, and the solutions for these problems were sought in the professional schools of education. Following passage of the Smith-Hughes Act in 1917, a widespread program of vocational education was developed. In the next quarter of a century, vocational education became increasingly important, and advocates of a liberal education in the traditional sense had to yield an important place in the curriculum to the newer vocational studies and activities.

The area of industrial education and manual training had been restricted, in the School of Pedagogy, to one course in 1910 and three in 1915. Of the latter three, two dealt with industrial education for defective children. General instruction in industrial arts appeared first at the elementary level in 1925. The course was entitled *The Industrial Arts in Connection with Children's Activities in the Elementary Grades*. One year earlier the Department of Secondary Education listed a course entitled *Introduction to Vocational Education*. Instruction was offered in

[2] *Annual Report* of the dean to the chancellor for 1927–28, pp. 75–76.

the theory, principles, practices, and problems in industrial arts education, industrial-technical education, and in vocational education.

The real impetus to expanding the work in this area came after establishment of a Department of Vocational Education in 1928. For sometime, staff members in industrial-technical and industrial arts education had entered into negotiations with the New York state education department, and by 1928 a Department of Vocational Education was added.

Through this department the School of Education concluded a mutually advantageous arrangement with the New York state education department which had been under negotiation during several previous years. This cooperative venture was effective in two ways: (1) it provided the training necessary in vocational education for the secondary school teaching positions in this area, and (2) by planning the program to be offered with the personnel at the state education department, successful completion of the program practically guaranteed issuance of a license. This is revealed by Withers in his annual report for the year 1925–26, in which the following references are made to these arrangements:

The development of the Department of Vocation Education . . . was extremely gratifying. A plan of cooperation was worked out between the Division of Vocational and Extension Education in the State Department of Education at Albany, and the School of Education of New York University, whereby the School of Education agreed to offer those courses which are required by the State Department for the supervisor's certificate in part-time education and in trade and industrial education.

The professional examination of the organization and administration of the continuation and part-time school became areas for study in the departmental offerings of secondary education as early as 1924–25. Following the formal departmentalization of industrial-technical and vocational education, these topics were given greater and more detailed consideration.

The development of the continuation and part-time schools coincided with the increased opportunities for students at minimum legal age to secure working papers permitting them to accept part-time employment while completing their secondary education. These schools were set up to meet the problems connected with the adjustment of programs and other activities to meet the particular needs of this group. The preparation of personnel trained to handle the administrative and teaching techniques unique to these institutions was the objective of these courses.

The arrangement with the state education department permitted the School of Education to equate the 480 hours of the industrial training program conducted by the state as 32 points of college credit. The authorization to convert these industrial training courses to the equivalent of the freshman year attracted at least five hundred individuals to the School of Education to take advantage of this opportunity to earn the bachelor's degree. The head of the Department of Vocational Education, Dr. Ralph E. Pickett, also was successful in securing the first approved four-year curriculum in industrial arts which previously had been given only at the Oswego and Buffalo State Normal Schools.

During these formative years, 1921–28, the major emphasis in the work of this department appeared to be placed on the theoretical and administrative problems of the area rather than on the experiential through shop activity. The relative recency of these subjects in the secondary school curriculum and the sudden expansion of activity stimulated by increased federal aid, in all probability, created the need for putting the discipline firmly on its feet before curricular refinements could be undertaken. Toward the close of this period, this department also supervised the first courses offered in homemaking. As this work underwent greater refinements, the scattered courses dealing largely with the organization and administration of homemaking in the high school were concentrated in a Department of Homemaking and Home Economics. After 1928 every branch of the homemaker's art was included, from baking to textiles.

The Systematizing of the Managerial Aspects of Education

By the turn of the century it had become apparent that the problems involved in the efficient management of education were becoming increasingly complex. Greater numbers of students and changing functions of the schools were making management more difficult and expert management essential. Administrative problems involved in centralization of these duties demanded attention. As a result of educational surveys and the adaptation of certain principles of business management to school management, a body of literature developed which opened the way for the systematic training of educational administrators.

In the light of his own professional orientation, it is not surprising to find that Withers assumed a large part of the instructional duties in the field of administration and supervision. Having come to New York University from the school superintendency of St. Louis where he had had professional association with W. T. Harris, Withers apparently was interested in introducing into the program of the School of Education elements of the most recent developments in school administration.

It will be recalled that the growth and development of this phase of education were found to be among the critical issues of the times. Therefore, response to this cultural pressure was found to be immediate in the newly organized teacher-education division at New York University.

In 1921, the initial year of operation, the School of Education bulletin listed two courses in administration which represented holdovers from the program of the School of Pedagogy. Two courses in supervision were added in this first year.

A rapid growth in the range of this department's offerings occurred in the next seven years. Not only was training in school financing and plant management opened up, but the conduct of school surveys was made a part of the administrator's background. The influence of the progressive movement in education was reflected in the work of this department in such courses as the *School Plant*. Here, attention was given to redesigning school buildings with especial reference to the classrooms. The relation of the state to education in matters of school management was brought into consideration, and by 1928 the range of offerings was calculated to provide preparation for administrative service from state commissioners of education to supervising principals in rural school districts. The tools of research were introduced, and such courses as *Use of Tests and Measurements in Educational Research, Methods and Techniques of Educational Research,* and *Elementary and Advanced Statistics* were added to the program.

In 1925 the first courses in personnel work were given in the Department of Administration and Supervision. Two years later, the demand for professional training in counseling and guidance and personnel administration had grown sufficiently to warrant incorporation of this work as an autonomous unit. Therefore, courses in this area, formerly listed under the Department of Administration and Supervision, were transferred to the Department of Personnel Administration and additonal courses added to cover the field from dormitory and social hall management to research in personnel problems.

The Establishment of Subject Matter Departments

In addition to response to specific social determinants, the program of the School of Education of New York University was influenced by a strong desire on the part of the administration and the faculty to explore new patterns of professional education.

The relations with other units of the University which had been established during the tenure of the School of Pedagogy were still in existence at the time of the transformation to the School of Education. Specifically, this relationship required matriculants in the teacher-education division to fulfill the liberal arts requirement in the program by taking such courses in the liberal arts college of the University. A similar arrangement existed between the School of Education and the School of Commerce with regard to content work in commercial subjects such as shorthand, typewriting, and office practice. These affiliations were maintained until 1928.

In 1928, by action of the University Council, certain "content" departments were authorized in the School of Education which made it possible for degree candidates to receive all of their training in the school in which they were matriculants. Two important considerations entered into these decisions: (1) upon its reorganization in 1921, the School of Education had been granted authority to offer the bachelor of science, master of arts, and doctor of philosophy degrees and to recommend its own candidates for them. This opportunity, in the eyes of the dean and his staff, imposed serious responsibility upon them for the conduct and quality of the instruction. (2) To meet this responsibility, it appeared mandatory that the School of Education should enjoy greater autonomy in evolving its philosophy and formulating its program than had been the case with the School of Pedagogy. The faculty, it appears, found it increasingly difficult to defend the complete divorce of content from method which was the existing situation. This position is made clear in a report of the Committee on Curricula (sic) Revision and Adjustment which was presented to and approved by the faculty on January 16, 1927. The report stated: "The curriculum is concerned with the "why" and the "how" as well as with the "what;" that is to say, content cannot be discussed fruitfully apart from its function and the conduct and administration of courses."

In touching upon a rationale for the integration of course content and methodology, the dean noted:

> We are not primarily interested . . . in the tracing of fact to fact relationships in a given subject, but rather in the tracing of fact to purpose relationships. . . . On account of the nature of the purposes which we are seeking to realize, we often find it necessary to cut across subject matter boundaries in search of the facts that we need.

The Council authorization resulted in the addition of five subject-matter departments including commerical education,[3] english, mathematics, science education, and social studies. Such authorization gave to these departments the dual role of (a) teaching content to all education majors and (b) training teachers of these subjects.

The importance of cultural areas such as art and music was acknowledged by the establishment of a Department of Music Education in 1925 and a Department of Art Education in 1926. In addition to art and music, which were among the newer specialties in the secondary school curriculum, the School of Education already had added

[3] Reference has been made to the cooperation between the State Department of Education and the Department of Vocational Education in the matter of upgrading certification requirements. Two announcements which point up similar reciprocal relations between the School of Education and the New York City Board of Education were made in this period: one indicated that, "Any one or more of the methods courses may be accepted by the Board of Education in fulfillment of requirements for teaching commercial subjects in New York City." A second announces recognition by the Board of Examiners of New York City of methods courses toward either a promotion or high school license in commercial subjects. *Bulletin*, School of Education, 1923–24, p. 46.

a Department of Religious Education in 1924 and announced the addition of a Department of Physical Education in 1925. Upon the opening of a camp site on which to carry forward graduate work in physical education, the dean noted that such a plan was a distinctive feature in the work of the School of Education. He also called attention to the fact that, in addition to preparing experts to guide the normal growth and development of young people, this department was prepared to train special experts to deal with handicapped cases.

Besides the education departments at the elementary and secondary levels, higher education was given attention through the Department of Normal School and Teachers College Education and a Department of College Education intended to prepare subject-matter teachers in colleges and teachers colleges.

Table III, pages 110–116, presents the growth of departments and course offerings in the School of Education of New York University between 1921 and 1929, the year of the founding of each department, and the name of the first head. It will be observed that, from seven departments offering sixty courses in 1921, the School of Education grew to twenty-two departments offering 420 courses in 1928.

RESUMÉ

One or more departments in the School of Education indicated response to the five issues selected for their cultural impact during the formative years of the School of Education.

Although the preparation of well-qualified teachers was

at all times a primary objective in the School of Education, this objective was never narrowly conceived. After 1921 there was a continuing evidence of the acceptance of the importance of the work of the professional school regardless of the area in which they served. Thus, the programs in the School of Education were designed to assist individuals to reach their fullest development and to achieve their maximum potential. Consequently, the School of Education program extended far beyond the preparation of classroom teachers. Several steps were taken in the first eight years of the institution to develop and introduce this concept. This newly conceived role may be considered in two broad categories: (1) the opening of training opportunities for new types of educational service and (2) the widening of the periphery of professional concern beyond the classroom. The following program changes may be noted in relation to these two categories.

Extension of Training Opportunities

As the curricula in the School of Education were adjusted to meet the social and professional needs of the period following World War I, one of the first steps taken was to establish programs for the preparation of men and women to teach in new areas such as industrial-technical education, commercial education, art education, music education, physical education, and religious education. The normal schools and teachers colleges generally did not offer training in these fields. Professional preparation also was available for individuals who wished to qualify in the various administrative and counseling posts,

TABLE III

GROWTH OF DEPARTMENTS AND COURSE GROUPINGS IN THE
SCHOOL OF EDUCATION OF NEW YORK UNIVERSITY

1921-22—1928-29

Legend

* First listing
† Previously combined in a single department
‡ Dropped Educational Research from title
∥ Term Teachers College added to dept. designation
Term Health added to department designation

Year	Tot. No. for Year	Designation	First Head	No. Crs. Offered	Tot. Crs. for Year
1921–22	7	Philos. and Hist. of Educ.	Herman Harrell Horne	10	
		Sch. Admin. and Supv.	John W. Withers	4	
		Experimental Ed.Ed. Research	Paul R. Radosavljevich	7	
		Psychology	James E. Lough	9	
		Elementary Ed.	Margaret E. Noonan	10	
		Secondary Ed.	P. W. L. Cox	16	
		Gen'l Theory of Edu. (Cluster of non-departmental courses)		4	60
1922–23	7	Philos. and Hist. of Educ.		10	

TABLE III (Cont.)

Year	Tot. No. for Year	Designation	First Head	No. Crs. Offered	Tot. Crs. for Year
		Sch. Adm. and Supv.		10	
		Experim. Ed. and Ed. Res.		6	
		Psychology		15	
		Elementary Educ.		17	
		Secondary Educ.		17	
		General Theory of Educ.	E. George Payne	7	82
1923–24	11	*Educ. Sociology		9	
		Elementary Educ.		17	
		Secondary Educ.	Charles E. Benson	18	
		*Educ. Psychology		13	
		‡Experimental Educ.		6	
		†{Philosophy of Educ.		4	
		History of Educ.		3	
		†{Educ. Administration		4	
		Supervision of Instruction		2	
		General Theory of Educ.		6	
		*Methods in Commercial Educ. (A group of courses listed under this heading in the Dept. of Secondary Educ.)		10	92

TABLE III (Cont.)

Year	Tot. No. for Year	Designation	First Head	No. Crs. Offered	Tot. Crs. for Year
1924–25	14	Educ. Sociology		8	
		Elementary Educ.		20	
		Secondary Educ.		27	
		Educ. Psychology		14	
		Experimental Educ.		5	
		Philosophy of Educ.		3	
		History of Educ.		5	
		Educational Admin.		7	
		Supervision of Instr.		3	
		*Religious Educ.	Wm. L. Thompson	1	
		*Normal Sch. Educ.	Ambrose L. Suhrie	5	
		*General Theory of Educ.		2	
		*General Subjects (Cluster of Non-depart. academic courses)		11	
		Methods in Commercial Educ.		8	119
1925–26	15	Educ. Sociology		15	
		Elementary Educ.		20	
		Secondary Educ.		32	
		Educ. Psychology		13	
		Experimental Educ.		5	
		Philosophy of Educ.		6	

TABLE III (Cont.)

Year	Tot. No. for Year	Designation	First Head	No. Crs. Offered	Tot. Crs. for Year
		History of Educ.		4	
		Educ. Administration		13	
		Supervision of Instruc.		3	
		Religious Education		2	
		Normal School Educ.		9	
		*Physical Educ.	C. W. Hetherington	39	
		*Music Educ.	Hollis Dann	20	
		General Subjects		16	
		Gen. Theory of Educ.		11	208
1926–27	17	Ed. Adminis.		16	
		*Art Educ.	Robt. A. Kissack	4	
		Supervision of Instruc.		4	
		Educ. Sociology		23	
		Elementary Educ.		15	
		Secondary Educ.		45	
		Educ. Psychology		15	
		Experimental Educ.		5	
		Philosophy of Educ.		3	
		History of Educ.		3	
		Religious Educ.		0	
		[Tchrs. Coll. & Normal Sch. Ed.		12	

TABLE III (Cont.)

Year	Tot. No. for Year	Designation	First Head	No. Crs. Offered	Tot. Crs. for Year
		Physical Educ.		36	
		Music Educ.	John O. Creager	67	
		*College Educ.		3	
		General Subjects		11	
		Gen. Theory of Educ.		6	268
1927–28	21	Admin. and Supv.		15	
		Art Educ.		6	
		College Educ.		3	
		*Commercial Educ.	Paul S. Lomax	13	
		Ed. Psychology		19	
		Ed. Sociology		17	
		Elementary Educ.		7	
		*English	Howard R. Driggs	16	
		Experimental Ed.		5	
		History of Educ.		3	
		*Mathematics	J. Andrew Drushel	8	
		Music Educ.		68	
		Normal Sch.-Tchs. Coll. Ed.		16	
		*Personnel Adminis.	Anna Y. Reed	7	
		Philosophy of Educ.		3	
		Physical Educ.		48	

TABLE III (Cont.)

Year	Tot. No. for Year	Designation	First Head	No. Crs. Offered	Tot. Crs. for Year
		*Science Educ. (First Head apptd. following year)		6	
		Secondary Educ.	Charles M. Gill	22	
		*Social Studies		7	
		*Vocational Educ.	Ralph E. Pickett	14	
		Gen. Theory of Ed.		4	307
1928–29	22	Ed. Admin. & Supv.		13	
		Art Educ.		12	
		College Ed.		1	
		Commercial Educ.		21	
		*Creative Educ.	Hughes Mearns	6	
		Ed. Psychology		25	
		Ed. Sociology		17	
		Elem. Educ.		13	
		English		26	
		Experimental Ed.		5	
		History of Educ.		10	
		*Home-Mdg., Home Eco. Ed.	Freda J. G. Winning	32	
		Mathematics		9	
		Music Educ.		68	
		Personnel Admin.		11	

TABLE III (Cont.)

Year	Tot. No. for Year	Designation	First Head	No. Crs. Offered	Tot. Crs. for Year
		Philosophy of Ed.		5	
		Physical Ed. & Health	Charles J. Pieper	44	
		Science		10	
		Secondary Ed.		33	
		Social Studies		18	
		Teachers Coll. Norm. Sch. Ed.		24	
		Vocational Educ.		17	420

the demands for which were growing throughout the country.

In pushing forward these academic frontiers, three things were accomplished: (1) the School of Education extended studies in individual growth and development. (2) It brought formerly isolated agencies (such as community) within the framework of education as a social institution. (3) It extended the sphere of influence of the School of Education in a more sharply defined consideration of the welfare of society as well as the welfare of the individual.

Chief Strengths of the Program 1921–28

Perhaps the most immediately observable characteristics of the program during the formative years were those of pioneering and innovation. Traditional barriers were broken down and opportunities provided for extending the participation of the professional school in the national welfare.

The provision of a major portion of instruction in evening and Saturday hours represented a significant advantage for an urban student body largely employed but eager to continue professional preparation.

Through the addition of new courses as well as the revitalizing of existing ones, the School of Education contributed to study and analysis of the structure, as well as the function of American education at all levels.

The incorporation of a study of social institutions other than the school pointed up the interaction and reciprocal relations between them and education.

Courses in history and philosophy of education were

accepted as fundamental to the development of critical thinking. Such courses were accepted as basic to the study of pedagogy and were required of all students, especially at the graduate level.

From the beginning, research and experimentation were considered significant and essential facets of the work of the institution. The importance of these disciplines were not overlooked in the program of the School of Education.

Its responses to the major issues of the times, together with the incorporation of an academic departure whereby a balanced program of liberal-cultural and professional courses was offered under the sole auspices of the teacher-education unit, suggest a concerted effort on the part of the faculty and administration of the School of Education to pioneer in the improvement of the profession of teacher education as well as to work for the continued upgrading of teacher qualifications.

Chief Weaknesses of the Programs 1921–28

There is a consensus in professional literature that, beginning in the 1920s, a great source of waste lay in too much duplication and overlapping of courses in education in the nation at large. Proliferation, too, developed in this era. Along with the expansion of course offerings there was subdividing of departments which stimulated the creation of additional courses. Further, while many subjects were added, few were dropped. Once a unit of instruction was added to the curriculum, a vested interest evolved which tended to resist attack.

These trends are discernible in the expanding program of the School of Education.

The tendency to proliferate, resulting in a form of internal duplication, together with a thinning out of course content, was most evident in the Department of Physical Education.

This department shared with the Departments of Educational Sociology, Educational Psychology, and Secondary Education, the charge of overlapping courses. Value was questioned where students were enrolled in such similar courses in several departments.

In some instances, course titles alone make proliferation discernible, as for example in the following:

Methods of Teaching Physical Training in Elementary Schools, Junior, and Senior High Schools
Methods of Teaching Physical Training in Junior and Senior High Schools
High School Methods in Physical Education

Examples of overlapping or duplication are:

From the bulletin for 1925–26:
  Education in Health Department of Educational Sociology, p. 72
  Teaching Health Department of Physical Education, p. 119
  Sociological Basis of Vocational Education Department of Educational Sociology, p. 75
  (Course description states: "This course will seek to determine the social basis of vocational education.")
  Theory, Principles, Practices, and Problems of Vocational Education Department of Secondary Education, p. 89
  (Course description states: "Some of the topics

> treated will be the history and the sociological foundations of vocational education.")

From the bulletin for 1926–27:

> *Social Behavior*   Department of Educational Sociology, p. 93
> (Course description includes the following: ". . . reviews the biological and psychological theories of personality.")
> *Social Psychology*   Department of Educational Psychology, p. 115
> (Description includes statement: ". . . studies the individual as a social unit.")
> *Mental Hygiene*   Department of Educational Psychology, p. 115
> *Sociological Basis of Mental Hygiene*   Department of Educational Sociology, p. 74

From this same bulletin, under the listings for the Department of Physical Education, again it is difficult to find clearly differentiated content or method in three courses entitled *Teaching Dancing-Men, Elementary Dancing,* and *Intermediate Dancing,* inasmuch as folk, national, character, and classical dances are indicated as the course content in the descriptions of all three courses on bulletin pages 135–36.

Finally, in the description of the course *Teaching of the Activities of Little Children* in the same bulletin and under the same department, it is stated that the course is a study of physical education activities of children below nine years of age. For the course *Teaching the Activities of Pre-adolescent Children,* among the same listings, there appears to be repetition since reference is made to "children below nine years of age to the late adolescent years." These descriptions were found in the bulletin, 1926–27, pages 156–57.

In spite of these apparent weaknesses, in less than a decade the teacher-training unit became the teacher-education division, organizing its instruction under twenty-two departments and offering 420 courses. The program represented an attempt on the part of the new teacher-education unit to do four things:

1] meet the contemporary social challenges,

2] build a program which would maintain a balance between the professional and the liberal arts courses,

3] bring both breadth and depth to the instructional areas covered, and

4] maintain a spirit of vision and courage to pioneer.

PERSONNEL

Educational leadership has been defined as representing vision, statesmanship, and growth. If the leader in education must be a scholar, must endeavor to keep abreast of changes in educational theory and practice, and must strive to comprehend the relationships of the school to the ever changing social structure, then these criteria may be applied to a consideration of the personnel of the School of Education in an endeavor to assess their contributions to the improvement of education and, particularly, teacher education.

Some evidence of leadership on the part of Dean Withers may be seen in the growth of the institution in staff, program, and student body. Having come to New York University from St. Louis, Withers looked to that locale for many of those he invited to join him in the challenging venture in New York University at Washington Square. The practice of seeking staff from the midwest region persisted for many years. Withers drew about him men and women who had had experience as teachers at all levels and as administrators.

With limitations imposed on the salaries he could offer new staff, the Dean proposed as an added inducement the opportunity for those who did not have advanced graduate degrees to work for the doctorate with tuition remission guaranteed. In quite a few cases these men and women took advantage of the opportunity to combine experience in a university environment with postgraduate work. This plan was fruitful in three ways:

1] It attracted individuals already familiar with dimen-sions the dean sought to add to the new program.

2] It provided such persons the incentive and the means for continuing their graduate education.

3] It built up the number of staff members holding a doctor's degree.

Of the twenty-two department chairmen functioning in the School of Education between 1921 and 1928, twelve held a doctor's degree at the time of their appointment, four did not and chose not to earn the advanced degree, and six earned the doctorate at New York University. Of those who had the doctorate before coming to the School of Education, two had earned the doctor of philosophy degree in foreign universities.

The First Faculty

When John W. Withers took up his administrative duties at Washington Square, he found a faculty comprised of five professors and nine lecturers or instructors. The five individuals holding academic rank were:

Herman Harrell Horne	Professor of the History of Education and of the History of Philosophy
James Edwin Lough	Professor of Experimental Psychology and Methods; Head of the Department of Psychology
Robert MacDougall	Professor of Descriptive Psychology
Margaret E. Noonan	Professor of Elementary Education
Paul Rankov Radosavljevich	Professor of Experimental Pedagogy

Four of the professors represented in their respective areas basic disciplines which traditionally were found in the teacher-training program. These were Horne, in history of education and history of philosophy; Lough and MacDougall, in branches of psychology; and Noonan, in elementary education. Such work as that of Radosavljevich, in experimental education (for which he had prepared in part by study with the celebrated pioneer in anthropology, Meumann), was not universally found in programs of pedagogy. It may be construed as evidence of the foresight of the administration of the School of Pedagogy that this field was introduced as early as 1910 with the appointment of Radosavljevich to the faculty of that school.

Horne, who came to the School of Pedagogy in 1908, achieved note in American education in two ways. The first was through his exposition of the philosophy of idealism in such works as *The Philosophy of Education* (1904), *Idealism and Education* (1910), *Free Will and Human Responsibility* (1912). Later, he became one of the interpreters and evaluators of the philosophy of John Dewey. Following the appearance of Dewey's *Democracy and Education*, Horne prepared two critical works entitled *This New Education* (1931) and *The Democratic Philosophy of Education* (1932). Of differing philosophers of education, Meyer states in *An Educ. Hist. of the Am. People*:

> If the Realists have failed to give much attention to modern pedagogy, then the Idealists, for their part, have given an immense amount. Of contemporary thinkers on the subject they clearly have the oldest tradition, for traces of their ideas can be seen in Plato. Unlike Pragmatism, moreover, Idealism has its protagonists in virtually every civilized land. In America they have been fairly numerous, and among educators some have even attained a high eminence, as witness William T. Harris, Josiah Royce, and Herman Harrell Horne. Of these worthies, the latter has given the Pragmatists their hardest tussle, not only by the sheer quantity of his output, but also by the appeal of his arguments.

Additions to the Staff Between 1921 and 1929

In consonance with the contemplated expansion of the role and function of the School of Education, the dean began the task of securing a corps of educators expert in the new dimensions which were to be added to the teacher-training program.

As had been recommended by Dean Balliet, of the School of Pedagogy, in 1917 in his predictions relating to the future development of education, Withers drew about him men and women who had had considerable experience as teachers in the elementary and secondary schools and, in certain instances, as administrative officers at the various educational levels. A number of the new appointees came from the Midwest, especially from St. Louis, Missouri where Withers had had his earlier experiences and in most instances had had professional contact with the individuals he now sought to build into a strong faculty for the young and vigorous teacher-training institution.

From its beginning, the program of the School of Education was conceived broadly within three categories: liberal-cultural, broad professional, and areas of specialization. These categories are reflected in faculty appointments within the first decade of the institution's founding. With no sense of adequately representing these persons, but to indicate them by name and area of interest, the roster included among others:

(1922) *E. George Payne* who was brought on from the presidency of the Harris Teachers College in St. Louis to introduce work in educational sociology. He later served as assistant dean and subsequently dean of the School of Education.

(1923) *Charles E. Benson* was assigned to effect the transition from pure psychology which had been the emphasis in the School of Pedagogy to educational psychology which had been given precedence in teacher training through the scientific movement in education.

Philip W.L. Cox, one of the leading participants in the national junior high school movement, was appointed to introduce the new studies at this level into the program and to reorganize the work of the department of secondary education in the light of the contemporary pressures.

Howard R. Driggs, an outstanding authority on America's early history and folklore (with special reference to this nation's pioneer trails), approached his task of building the courses in English education with the view of making the subject vital to the elementary and secondary school pupils through the utilization of this country's rich and colorful lore.

(1924) *Paul S. Lomax* planned the work in commercial education so that by the end of this formative period (1928) those specializing in this field could receive their total training in the School of Education without the necessity of attending another division of the University in order to acquire skill in the subject which they wished to teach.

(1924) *Charles M. Gill* was first appointed as assistant professor of the teaching of history and geography. When subject-matter departments were authorized in 1927, he became the first chairman of the newly created Social Studies Department.

Milton Early Loomis had taught courses in political science and government in the Liberal Arts College of New York University when he was invited by Dean Withers to become a professor of education in the School of Education. He subsequently served as assistant dean and for several years as director of the summer school.

Ralph E. Pickett coordinated the work in vocational education including the areas of industrial arts and technical education. Through his efforts and cooperation with the New York State Department of Education the program in the School of Education was among the first developed to meet changing certification requirements and the requirements for new supervisor's certificates. Dr. Pickett served as assistant director of the Institute of Education and for a period of thirty years as secretary of the faculty. Dr. Pickett served as chairman of the Department of Vocational Education from the year of its official establishment (1927 through 1947). He also became assistant dean and associate dean in the School of Education.

Two additional appointments in 1924 were those of *Anna Y. Reed,* who brought formal study of personnel administration into the Department of Administration and Supervision and later served as chairman of the Department of Personnel Administration, and *Ambrose L. Suhrie* whose teaching brought into the program of the School of Education concern for teacher preparation beyond the elementary and secondary levels. The introduction of this work represented an innovation in the field of pedagogy in this era.

(1925)   In this year appointments were made to three distinctive areas which served to enrich the School's growing program:

Hollis E. Dann, who had served as head of the music department at Cornell University and as state director of music for Pennsylvania, was called to organize the Department of Music Education. The work of this department, under Dann and his competent staff, brought large enrollments of those who sought to qualify for the new positions then opening up in elementary and secondary schools and who did not find a comparable program easily available. The department gained national recognition and became one of the outstanding departments of its kind in the country.

Hughes Mearns already had established a reputation at the Lincoln School of Teachers College for his ability to free and encourage self-expression in children. His courses attracted a wide clientele throughout the tenure of his chairmanship of the department.

With the appointment of *Clark W. Hetherington* in 1925 and *Jay B. Nash* in 1926, the Department of Physical Education was organized and developed to the point where it became subsequently one of the largest and most outstanding departments in the country. The addition of a summer camp for graduate work in physical education added to the reputation for leadership in this field.

(1926) A new dimension in teacher training was added to the program of the School of Education when, in this year, a Department of Art Education was set up under the chairmanship of *Robert A. Kissack*. Kissack also served for a period as director of the Institute of Education and was instrumental in making available to outlying communities some of the first courses in art education.

John O. Creager came from the deanship of the College of Education of the University of Arizona to set up one of the early programs in teacher-training institutions devoted to the training of teachers of academic subjects in colleges and universities.

J. Andrew Drushel was appointed in this year to initiate work in mathematics and later to organize a Department of Mathematics in the School of Education. Drushel was known to the dean through his work in the Harris Teachers College, St. Louis, Missouri and through his co-authorship (with Withers and Mathilda C. Gecks) of a widely used series of textbooks in mathematics.

(1928) *Charles J. Pieper* was added to the staff as chairman of the newly created Department of Science Education and Professor *Robert K. Speer* assumed the chairmanship of the Department of Elementary Education.

This list does not represent the total faculty appointments during these formative years. However, the individuals named served as the major faculty members who, in most instances, became the first chairmen of their respective departments. Their selection for specific reference above was based on the following criteria:

1] They had achieved professional recognition prior to coming to New York University.

2] As observed through the departmental programs they established and directed, they served to implement the stated aims and objectives of the School of Education.

3] They were called to the School because of the unusual nature of their area of specialization and their consequent contributions to the enrichment of the program.

The major faculty was supplemented by additional personnel as they were needed. An interesting feature of these auxiliary appointees during these early years was the non-academic background of a considerable proportion of those in the categories of instructor or lecturer. The latter especially were predominately experts in highly specialized fields who were brought in either from business and industry or from other school assignments to give courses and laboratory or shop work for teachers in areas where, up to that time, no adequate number of trained teachers existed. This was true particularly in such departments as vocational education, home economics, music education and some of the newer phases of physical education such as adaptive work with the handicapped.

The success of the program, as shown by the phenomenal growth of the School of Education in its first decade, gives evidence of an appreciable degree of cooperation and cohesiveness in the instructional body. It may be assumed that the majority of these men and women shared the dean's pioneering spirit and indefatigable dedication to the forward movement in teacher education. Together with the dean, they represented an important segment of the avant-garde in contemporary philosophy relating to professional preparation for educational services.

Table IV, below, indicates the distribution of faculty

TABLE IV

DISTRIBUTION OF FACULTY BY NUMBER AND RANK
SCHOOL OF EDUCATION BETWEEN 1921 AND 1928

Year	Professor	Assoc. Prof.	Asst. Prof.	In- structor	Lecturer	Total
1921–22	6				11	17
1922–23	6		3		14	23
1923–24	9		2		19	30
1924–25	12	2	4	6	23	47
1925–26	15	3	12	15	24	69
1926–27	18	8	16	13	28	83
1927–28	15	8	16	22	27	88

members by number and rank in the School of Education between 1921 and 1928. From these data it will be observed that there was an increase of over 550 percent in the teaching staff during the period covered. The table also reveals that, within the professional appointments, full professorships exceeded the numbers of assistant and associate professorships throughout this decade.

Certain characteristics have stamped the faculty of the School of Education through these years of its growth and early development. For those interested in the persistence of institutional personality, it may be noted that the characteristics mentioned below by Withers as pertinent to the period under discussion have continued to be outstanding and have merited reference to the present time.

The Dean wrote: "The characteristic of the School of Education most frequently mentioned by our students is the friendly, human quality of the Faculty and the evident sincerity of purpose of all the members to be of real service to the students."

The Dean went on to state that the maintenance of this friendly spirit was essential to the continued development of the institution. He indicated, however, that this called for a type of work which would make heavy demands upon the School and upon the time of the teachers, and that:

The earnest endeavor of the Faculty to continue to merit the reputation thus gained and at the same time to take proper care of the more than 900 graduate students . . . has meant that each member of the staff has been forced to carry a heavier load than he should.

Within this quotation is seen at once both the positive reference to the quality of the faculty of the School of Education and the reflection of one of its most persistent issues, namely, the extraordinarily heavy demands made upon each member of the staff.

STUDENT BODY

Up to 1921 the enrollment of the School of Pedagogy consisted, in the main, of two classes of students: graduates of colleges matriculated for advanced degrees and graduates of normal schools or those who had completed two or three years of college work.

In 1922 the total student body of the School of Education was 221. By 1928 it had reached 4013. The factors that contributed to this extraordinary growth pattern were the following:

1] the increased demand for teachers fulfilling upgraded certification requirements, including college and university degrees,

2] the extension of education into new specializations and community services,

3] the growth of the metropolitan area,

4] the increased availability of late afternoon and Saturday courses, permitting students to pursue degrees on a part-time basis, and

5] the few competitive institutions of teacher education.

The introduction of undergraduate work in the School of Education, as well as the availability of undergraduate training in academic subjects, soon created a body of new students made up, not only of freshmen, but also of transfer students from normal schools who wished to round out their education and earn a college degree in the shortest period possible.

In 1924, upon recommendation of the faculty and authorization by the Council of the University, the School of Education was empowered to recognize two years of work in a normal school as 64 points, or half of the total requirement for an undergraduate degree in the School of Education. This made it possible for transfer students to earn a four-year baccalaureate degree in two years and proved a strong inducement for many to come to the institution.

Table V, page 134, relating to the growth of the student

body, reveals that for some years the undergraduate student body outnumbered the graduate group. The changing requirements in teacher certification and the upgrading of teachers noted for this period may be assumed to have had some influence on the situation. Further, although the system of graduate education entered a period of great growth and diversification following 1900, the peak activity in this domain in the School of Education came in the fourth decade of the twentieth century.

In addition to showing a phenomenal growth in the student body between 1921 and 1928, the data of Table V reflect a continuation of one pattern established in the School of Pedagogy, namely, the preponderance of females. This increased to a peak of 73.2 percent in the year 1927–28 among the undergraduates. Similar disparity between the sexes did not occur in the graduate body where the difference between the numbers of men and women never exceeded twenty and, in the two years 1924–25 and 1926–27, was reduced to a feminine lead of only four. The markedly greater proportion of undergraduate women may be indicative of certain cultural pressures including response to the mounting demands for secondary school teachers and the practical fact that low teachers' salaries dissuaded more and more men from electing teaching as a profession.

At the close of its initial year of operation, the School of Education was serving 221 students. Within its first decade this figure reached 4013 students, an increase of some 2000 percent. A proportion of this increase was due to the migration of students from the normal schools to

looks forward that for many years, the undergraduate
divided body outnumbered the graduate group. The
changing character of our civilization and the
importance of teachers indicated that period may be assumed to have had some influence on the situation.
During this period of graduate education received a period of great growth and organization following it, the peak activity in this domain in the School
of Education came in the fourth decade of the twentieth
century.

In addition to showing a phenomenal growth in the
student body between 1921 and 1928, the data of Table V
illustrate another important matter established in the
School of Education, namely, the preponderance of re-
males. This tended to persist throughout in the
past 1921, although the data show a marked change in disparity
between the sexes throughout the student body,
where the difference between the numbers of men and
women never exceeded twenty until the two years
1921-22, and after that exceeded large... lead of
male here. The remarkably steady fraction of undergraduate women may be... the increasing demand
for secondary school teachers... the... fact that
less teachers colleges demanded... and more interesting... electing teacher...

As the close of its initial year of operation, the School
of Education was serving 221 students. Within its first
decade this figure reached 4013 students, an increase of
nine-tenths... of this increase was due
to the major... from the annual schools to...

TABLE V
GROWTH AND DISTRIBUTION OF THE STUDENT BODY
SCHOOL OF EDUCATION
1921–28

Year	Undergraduate			Graduate			Totals		Total
	Men	Women	Total	Men	Women	Total	Men	Women	
1921–22	—	18	18	94	109	203	94	127	221
1922–23	92	190	282	86	102	188	198	292	480
1923–24	79	387	466	109	139	248	188	526	714
1924–25	157	636	793	196	200	396	353	836	1189
1925–26	261	1043	1304	295	231	526	556	1274	1830
1926–27	504	1513	2017	325	329	654	829	1842	2671
1927–28	726	2360	3086	450	477	927	1176	2837	4013

the colleges and universities, a shift less motivated, undoubtedly, by an unquenched thirst for knowledge than by a desire to qualify for more attractive and responsible positions. The demands of students were, therefore, responsible in part for the improvement in standards and for the extension of the period of study in teacher education.

As previously implied, the availability of evening and Saturday courses influenced enrollment to a considerable degree, since statistics reveal a dominance of sixty percent of evening and Saturday students over day-time students during the period of 1921–28.

The unprecedented growth of the student body, graphically demonstrated in Figure 1, page 136, placed a strain on the physical facilities of the institution that Withers regarded as a primary problem among those calling for speedy solution.

FACILITIES

Upon acceptance of the stewardship of the School of Education, Withers had found the staff of the teacher-training division sharing two rooms on the ninth floor of what is now called the University's Main Building, at 100 Washington Square East. The remaining space was rented to the American Book Company. There was an agreement between New York University and the New York state legislature that the building could be used partly for income-producing purposes and without payment of taxes by the University as long as *all* of the work of the Schools of Pedagogy and Law, and the executive offices of the University, was conducted in this edifice.

In an address to the faculty on September 28, 1925, the

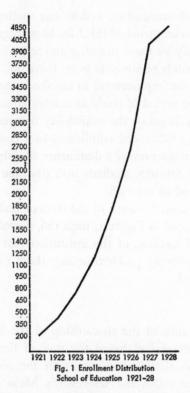

Fig. 1 Enrollment Distribution
School of Education 1921-28

subject of adequate facilities occupied the major part of
the dean's remarks. He referred to the urgency for securing, with the least possible delay, the buildings and equipment necessary to carry out effectively the contemplated
program and to complete the structural organization of
the School. The dean said, "If these necessary buildings
and equipment cannot be secured within the next twelve
or eighteen months, it will be impossible to attain the
success now hoped for, and even the ultimate realization

of our aims in any worthy way will be seriously in doubt."

A persistent threat to the continued growth of local pa-
tronage was seen by Withers, as it had been seen earlier
by Balliet, in the tuition-free city and metropolitan institutions which concurrently were enlarging their facilities
and extending their services along lines similar to those of
the School of Education. For this reason the facilities of
the School of Education had to be of such quality that
they would attract students from various parts of the
United States as well as from foreign countries. As a last
point on this matter the dean submitted that ". . . it is
impossible, no matter how strong and active the faculty
may be, to keep even the respect of our students with our
present lack of facilities in library, gymnasiums, laboratory
schools, etc."

In his 1924–25 annual report, Withers again referred
to the growing demands for expanded facilities. He
pointed out that:

By far the greatest difficulty experienced by the School of
Education during the year was that of meeting the need for
additional building accommodations due to the rapid growth
of the School of Education and of the other divisions of the
University located at Washington Square.

The dean went on to report that the offices of the
School of Education had to be transferred to rented quarters on the sixth floor of the Lies Building (located at
the corner of Washington Square East and West Fourth
Street) in order to provide for additional classroom space
in the Main Building. He pointed out that the desirable
development of the School would be ". . . greatly and
perhaps permanently retarded if more adequate accom-

modations for classrooms, laboratories, gymnasiums, and housing facilities for students cannot be secured at a very early date."

Early in 1925 the dean convinced the central University administration that an opportunity to acquire property adjacent to the Main Building could not be ignored. Accordingly, upon authorization, a movement was begun by the dean and some members of the faculty of the School of Education to organize a corporation to purchase certain properties at Washington Square and to hold them for the use of the University until it could secure sufficient funds to relieve this corporation of that responsibility. Options were secured on three pieces of property on the east side of Washington Square between Fourth Street and Washington Place. The corporation was legally organized and contracts were signed for the purchase of the property at a price of $899,100. Mortgages were already placed on the property to the total amount of $500,000, and it was decided to secure the remainder of the purchase money, $399,100, and enough additional funds to reduce the mortgage indebtedness to $355,000 by the sale of debenture bonds against the assets of the corporation. It was decided to lease the entire property to the University for a period of ten years for an annual rental sufficient to meet all expenses, including interest on the indebtedness and a sufficient amount to retire at least $10,000 in bonds annually.[3]

[3] Dean John W. Withers, interview in Bradenton, Florida, 1955. Information relating to the establishment of the School of Education Realty Corporation and its activities was secured in a personal interview and from records in the files of Associate Dean Pickett who served as secretary of the Corporation.

At a meeting of the faculty in July, 1925, at which this plan was presented, $100,000 worth of bonds were subscribed for. Two days later, at a meeting of the summer school students who were taking courses in education, approximately $75,000 additional bonds were sold. Two members of the Council of the University purchased $50,000 each. Subsequently, $125,000 worth of bonds were sold to the Corn Exchange Bank and $15,000 to the Fordham National Bank, and enough additional bonds were sold to current and former students of the School of Education and their friends to meet all the obligations of the corporation and complete the purchase.

The properties were purchased in August, 1925 with the understanding, among the faculty of the School of Education and the Council and central administration of the University, that as soon as financially possible a building should be erected on the site which would serve the needs of the School of Education. Plans were formulated for the erection of such a building which would include necessary office space, adequate provisions for classrooms, and also dormitory accommodations to provide for 900 students. A careful estimate of the income contemplated from the building indicated to the dean that, from this source alone, the building, in all probability, could be paid for within a period of fifteen years.

Architectural plans for the building were prepared by the firm of Schultze and Weaver and the cost estimated at nearly $4,000,000. The plan, as submitted, did not fully accord with the architectural plans of the University for the several divisions located at Washington Square.

Neither were the necessary funds for the erection of the building immediately available.

It was finally decided to take care, temporarily, of the need for office and classroom space by continuing the use of the property of the Realty Corporation with only one change. A small portion of the land was taken to complete a plot approximately 100 feet square at the northwest corner of Fourth and Greene Streets on which to erect a twelve-story building. This would meet the needs of special departments of the School of Education, such as music education and physical education, until such time as a satisfactory building could be erected on the remaining property owned by the Realty Corporation.

Architect James Gamble Rogers was requested to prepare and submit plans for this new building. These plans were accepted and erection of the building began immediately. This was made possible by the use of gifts to the University which were made chiefly by Mr. Percy Straus, Dr. William H. Nichols, and Dr. John P. Munn of the University Council. The building was completed and dedicated on February 28, 1930. The year 1930 ended the active period of the Realty Corporation. Its legal termination will be discussed in the succeeding chapter where changing facilities in the School of Education are treated.

AUXILIARY AGENCIES

Although they do not come within the central province of this project, two additional services closely related to the School of Education warrant mention at this point. These are the summer school and the Institute of Education.

Elsbree has commented on auxiliary agencies in the training of teachers. In his book, *The American Teacher: Evolution of a Profession in a Democracy,* he reported:

Two agencies, the summer school and university extension, both closely affiliated with colleges and universities, gradually supplanted the lyceum as an institution of serious study. . . .

With communities maintaining relatively short school years and long summer vacations, a golden opportunity existed to supply teachers with at least a part of the much-needed professional and academic training which educators and laymen had been so earnestly urging.

The Summer School

As early as 1894 New York University conducted summer courses at its uptown center including some of the work in pedagogy offered during the regular year in the School of Pedagogy at Washington Square.

Withers early recognized the potential value, to prospective teachers as well as teachers in service, of the availability of as wide a variety of courses as was feasible to offer during the time individuals were free to take advantage of this opportunity. By 1925 all of the work of the summer school was conducted at the Washington Square center and an extract from the summer school bulletin for 1925 indicates the extent of the program:

Courses in education designed for school executives and supervisors and for teachers in elementary schools, high schools, normal schools, and colleges. The departments of art, music, physical education, and methods in commercial education provide systematic training for teachers and supervisors of these subjects.

An additional advantage was provided as indicated by the following statement from the same catalogue:

In the undergraduate division of the School of Education, teachers who have completed a normal school or teachers college course of two years, in addition to a standard four-year high-school course, may begin a course in the Summer School leading to the bachelor's degree.

Finally, the summer work in 1926 inaugurated a unique experiment in bringing the study and practice of education into its most natural environment. This was the establishment of a summer camp on property leased from the Harriman State Park Commission, in the Palisades Interstate Park (at Lake Sebago, in Sloatsburg, New York), for graduate work in physical education. The initial idea of such a camp and the major part of the work involved in bringing it into reality came from the efforts of Dr. Jay B. Nash, the camp's first director. Dr. Nash succeeded Dr. Hetherington as chairman of the Department of Physical Education in 1926.

A special bulletin covering the work conducted at the camp states:

> One of the chief purposes for the establishment of the summer camp of the School of Education was to stimulate interest in the natural education that takes place in the out-of-doors.
> . . . .
> It will be possible for students to undertake work designed to train specialists in the field of physical education, both in the administration and supervision of school systems and teacher training institutions, surrounded by ideal camping conditions.

The dean reported to the chancellor that, if the plan of the summer school in camp was successful, it would be a distinctive feature in the work of the School of Education and a unique venture in teacher education.

The work and prestige of the summer session grew steadily, and the student body, largely graduate, was drawn from all parts of the continental United States as well as from many foreign lands.

The summer work offered through the School of Education may be assumed to have made three contributions to the field:

1] It permitted the completion of professional preparation in shorter time for those desiring to take advantage of summer study.

2] It made possible for students too distant from New York to attend the School of Education during the regular academic year to have the experience of study at a large, urban university in a cosmopolitan environment such as New York City provides.

3] It stimulated intercultural relationships and understanding among many different groups of students.

A further expansion came with an agreement reached in 1923 between the University and the Chautauqua Institute in western New York. Under this agreement the School of Education assumed supervision and direction of the summer courses in education at Chautauqua and arranged to credit these courses toward its degrees. The cooperative arrangement brought new students to the School of Education, raised to a higher academic level the general character of instruction at Chautauqua, and in other ways proved advantageous to both institutions. It carried the name of the University to an entirely new clientele. A complete analysis of the New York University summer session programs, together with an evaluation of their influence on American education warrants an independent research study.

The Institute of Education

A plan whereby teachers and others engaged in the profession of education throughout the United States may secure professional and general training under such conditions that work completed will be credited toward a degree in the School of Education.[4]

In view of the fact that there was a growing demand for the services of the faculty of the School of Education outside of Washington Square, it was decided to establish a new organization on a basis that would make it possible for this service to be rendered without violating the agreement with the New York state legislature (p. 135) which called for conduct of the instructional program of the School of Education at Washington Square.

Accordingly, a plan for an Institute of Education was submitted by Dean Withers to the Chancellor and the Council as part of the general scheme of reorganization submitted by him in 1924. This plan was approved, and the Institute of Education was established in the Fall of 1924.

The Institute provided for various types of services, among which were the following:

1] Courses were to be given for teachers, principals, supervisors, superintendents, and special workers in schools and colleges.

2] Educational research was to be conducted, including studies directed by regular members of the staff, in

[4] *Bulletin*, School of Education, 1924–1925, p. 19.

school systems desiring such service or where such service was available. Such research was intended to focus on the improvements of learning and the teaching process.

3] Comprehensive school surveys, involving analyses of conditions affecting progress of school systems, and recommendations related to financial, administrative, supervisory, and instructional needs were to be provided when desired.

4] Advisory relationships were to be available in which the services of individual members or committees of the faculty of the School of Education could be secured on special problems concerned with policy, program, organization, administration, or supervision of school work.

5] Conferences and lecture work were to be furnished for laymen through school board associations, women's clubs, civic orders, parent-teacher organizations, church clubs, and fraternal groups.

6] Teachers' conferences or Institute work was to be made available to assist in the planning of programs and to provide speakers for discussion of various school and civic problems.

The courses offered in the Institute of Education would be presented under conditions identical with those at Washington Square in terms of requirements for admission, course requirements, and faculty.

A portion of the time of regular faculty members would be set apart each year for this work, and the courses would be given by faculty members without additional salary except for the cost of transportation and $100 additional for each full course in order to provide for the extra time faculty members would be required to give in connection with transportation to and from the various institute centers. With courses offered as far away as Boston and Baltimore, it was necessary in some cases to use air transportation, and in those days this frequently meant traveling in open-cockpit monoplanes which gave rise to the local designation of these faculty members as the "flying professors."

A special announcement relating to the establishment of this educational unit states:

> The purpose of the Institute of Education . . . is not to provide a popular series of lectures on educational topics, nor merely to provide isolated courses in special subjects of local or passing interest. The object is to give . . . organized courses of study, leading to the ultimate attainment of baccalaureate and graduate degrees.

With reference to the relationship of the Institute of Education to established agencies, the special announcement made it clear that there was no intent on the part of the University to duplicate or compete with the work of other educational institutions but rather to cooperate with them and supplement the work of other agencies throughout the country having similar objectives. No center was established in any community without the approval of the responsible educational authorities in that community.

All the above plans were put into practice, and, until its dissolution in 1933 when the functions were transferred to a separate unit of the University called the Division of General Education, the Institute of Education represented a pioneer effort to provide professional service to any school or system which applied for such service as well as to make courses available in local areas under as nearly comparable conditions as possible to the conditions at the Washington Square campus. Such conditions included space, library facilities, any necessary additional equipment, and instructional staff. The work was carried on only where conditions made it impossible for a competent local college or university to render the service. Such service kept the members of the faculty of the School of Education in contact with teachers and school systems throughout the country.

As in the case of the summer school of the University, a detailed study of the Institute of Education is not provided in this research since, as a distinct entity it merits its own study, and since omission of detailed reference does not affect, per se, the present study of the School of Education at Washington Square.

SUMMARY

The years encompassed here, and referred to as the formative years of the School of Education, 1921–28, were among those which saw several significant developments in American education, including: (1) the expansion of the educational enterprise to include within its services most of the children and youth as well as a large part of the adult population; (2) the enrichment of the curriculum; (3) attempts to order the instructional program so as to give it system and coordination; (4) the development of new types of structural organization; (5) changing relations of government to education; and (6) more effective education of teachers. These transformations made possible the formulation of an educational science and the advancement of teacher education from practical training to professional preparation.

Reviewing the changes effected in the teacher-education division at New York University in this period, there is support for the conclusion that the reconstituted School of Education made a distinct contribution in forwarding these achievements.

The staff members, including the dean, were selected for competency in their special fields as well as for their acceptance of education as a dynamic force in American life.

The complete reorganization of the program of instruction is an illustration of a conviction, apparently shared by the faculty and the administration of the institution, that in the twentieth century the professional school had a responsibility to demonstrate leadership in the upgrading of the teaching profession.

To work toward effective implementation of its goals, the leadership in the School of Education indicated concern, not only for the contemporary social issues as reflected in the program, but for an efficient internal organization and an adequate physical environment in which to meet the social and education challenges of the times.

Growth was the keynote of the years 1921–28 in the School of Education. The faculty increased from fourteen members in 1921 to eighty-eight in 1928. In the same period course offerings grew from sixty to 420. Within this expansion can be observed innovations in areas of study added, such as creative education, educational sociology, vocational education, physical education, art education, music education, and the radical departure represented

The School of Education Building
dedicated February 28, 1930

in the placement of content, or subject-matter instruction, under the aegis of the school of the matriculant's choice.

Further, preparation was offered for those seeking to enter the fields of administration and guidance, then coming to the forefront in the educational organization.

That the efforts of the faculty and administration of the School of Education met with a measure of success may be observed from the phenomenal growth of the student body from 221 in 1921 to 4013 in 1928.

The School of Education had demonstrated its vigor and accomplishment during its formative years. It remained for the soundness and enduring characteristics of these accomplishments to be tested in the decade following when all educational institutions were faced with the unanticipated and serious consequences of a national crisis.

5 · The School of Education
in the Depression Years 1929–38

Hardly had the School of Education of New York University conceived its new role in the field of professional education when the nation suffered an economic collapse of catastrophic proportions. So devastating was this experience that several of the former cultural traditions of the nation failed to survive its impact.

For example, if one examines democracy in terms of its component elements, one finds an early tradition that the individual was expected to exploit the opportunities for achieving his material advancement without interference or assistance from government. Liberty and equality of opportunity had been broadly conceived in terms of protection against governmental encroachment. But, by the end of the 1930s, the concepts of liberty and equality included, not merely absence of restraint, but positive values which could be achieved only by government regulations. In this vein, Franklin D. Roosevelt, campaigning against Hoover in 1932, made clear his convictions that the day of unrestrained individualism had passed. In a speech before the Commonwealth Club of San Francisco, he stated:

A glance at the situation today only too clearly indicates that equality of opportunity as we have known it no longer exists. . . . All this calls for a reappraisal of values. . . . Our task now is not the discovery or exploitation of natural resources, or necessarily producing more goods. It is the soberer, less dramatic business of administering resources and plants already in hand . . . of distributing wealth and products more equitably, of adapting existing organizations to the service of the people.[1]

The passage of the Social Security Act in 1935 was evidence of this modification of the concept of individualism and of the newer attitude that the responsibility for what happened to the individual had to be shared by society. As for the abrupt liquidation of the paper profits of the bull stock market, this was a brutal demonstration of one grave shortcoming of American economic life: the absence of any functioning system of checks and balances. This situation led to a series of actions through governmental agencies. For example, out of the revelations of past transactions discovered by the Senate Committee on Banking and Finance, which created an overwhelming sentiment in favor of additional protection for investors, came ratification of the Securities and Exchange Act in 1934, and, in banking, federal supervision over the reserve system was widened and made more stringent.

The veil of laissez-faire which for so long had clouded the vision of the man in the street was rudely stripped

[1] *The Public Papers and Addresses of Franklin D. Roosevelt*, pp. 750–52.

away in the space of one short week in October, 1929, and the starkness of the reality which many individuals faced for the first time proved intollerable in hundreds of cases. The social and economic changes produced by the Depression affected the structure and operation of several American institutions, and education did not escape the tempest.

The Effect on Education Generally

The national catastrophe influenced three aspects of education: (1) the school population, (2) the teaching force, and (3) the curriculum.

THE SCHOOL POPULATION DURING
THE DEPRESSION

An immediate effect of the social disequilibrium was to prolong education for many who, under conditions of prosperity, would have gone to work after finishing the elementary school. Under widespread joblessness, the number of high school pupils grew from about 4,500,000 in 1929 to 6,000,000 in 1935, an increase of 33⅓ percent, and the trend continued. The prolonging of education, it may be assumed, better equipped youth for the economic struggle ahead, and, to this extent, many boys and girls profited from adversity.

The increase in enrollment and an attendant drop in the birthrate wrought a significant shift in the relative sizes of elementary and secondary populations. Between 1934 and 1936 the number of public high schools rose by 900, but elementary schools shrank by about 4000. At the same time, some fifty public and 200 private institutions of higher learning came into existence.

Between 1932 and 1939 the federal government participated in education affairs more than at any previous time in the nation's history. Indirectly, this participation took form through activities of certain of the "alphabetical agencies" created during the administration of Franklin D. Roosevelt. An example of this participation was the maintenance of some 1460 nursery schools under the Works Progress Administration. This same agency undertook the renovation of nearly 80,000,000 books, chiefly in school and public libraries.

Another federal venture created as an expediency to combat unemployment was the Civilian Conservation Corps. Its heavily patronized voluntary educational program and library facilities added to the value of the experience, and employers looked favorably on graduates of the corps.

Even the Tennessee Valley Authority, essentially an experiment in public utilities, sponsored a lively adult education movement which spread from the workers to the larger community. Further, under the Federal Economic Recovery Act of 1934 the National Youth Administration was established. This agency enrolled 630,000 in its two major programs. No fewer than seven-eighths of these were receiving student aid, and the remainder were employed on out-of-school projects. Vocational guidance programs sent many boys into manual workshops and girls into domestic science classes. The much larger group of beneficiaries, nearly 2,000,000 in all, were high school and college students who needed financial aid to continue their education.

THE TEACHING FORCE

Teachers suffered serious setbacks during the Depression years, streaming out into the ranks of the unemployed in great numbers. Where positions were maintained, many were paid in scrip, as in Chicago, and, in other instances, payments were delayed over varying lengths of time. In 1932 only forty percent of those completing teacher-education programs obtained employment.

One result of the lack of employment of teachers caused by the Depression was the extension of academic preparation on the part of those who were unemployed. Many returned to institutions of higher learning to enrich their professional backgrounds, looking toward improved employment opportunities in the future.

A wave of chauvinism had begun to sweep over the nation in the previous decade, gathered full strength during the 1930s, and had serious implications both for the teaching force and the curriculum. Here the target was "unpatriotic" school books and "suspect" educators.

The whole question of academic freedom was further stirred up by a rider attached to the District of Columbia appropriations bill passed by Congress in June 1935. This bill provided funds for the District of Columbia, including appropriations for the public schools. The rider, commonly but not favorably known as "the little red rider," stated: "Hereafter no part of any appropriation for the public schools shall be available for the payment of the salary of any person teaching or advocating communism.[2]

Before receiving their salaries, teachers and officers in the District of Columbia were required to sign a statement swearing that they had not at any time within a given pay period taught or advocated communism. This and similar practices were introduced in many other communities.

In June 1935 a memorandum on academic freedom was issued by the research division of the National Education Association. The position taken was that teachers should have the privilege of presenting all points of view, including their own, on controversial issues without danger of reprisal by the school administration or by pressure groups in the community. The general reaction of serious educators to this intensive drive against implied subversion in the schools is reflected in a resolution adopted by the council of the American Historical Association which stated:

. . . the clearly implied charges that many of our leading scholars are engaged in treasonable propaganda and that tens of thousands of American school teachers and officials are so stupid or disloyal as to place treasonable text-books in the hands of children, is inherently and abviously absurd.

Nevertheless, the threats to academic freedom represented by such charges and by the growing numbers and varieties of loyalty oaths demanded of teachers caused many members to leave the schools, never to return.

[2] A. F. Myers and C. O. Williams, *Education in a Democracy*, pp. 248–49.

THE CURRICULUM

The stock market crash in 1929 heightened awareness of the extent to which corruption in business and industry had contributed to the economic collapse. The national disillusionment which followed found expression in a sharper concern for better training in citizenship and in the social sciences generally. This task was bestowed upon the schools; hence, the period was marked by a substantial increase in the social studies at both the secondary and higher levels of education.

During the darkest days of the Depression there sprang up all over the country various organizations which were pressure groups in a very real sense. Their watchword was economy and their numbers included the National Economy League, taxpayers leagues, certain state chambers of commerce, the National Association of Manufacturers, and similar organizations. Their idea of economy was to eliminate certain educational services, shorten school years, reduce teachers' salaries, and close schools. Adolphe E. Meyer has pointed out that while the Depression lay heaviest upon the South, its shadow was everywhere. In regard to curtailment of elimination of educational services, he has stated: ". . . Specialties like art and music, and even shop work and kindergartens, came under the ax. . . . By 1933 the education of a round ten million children was crippled." [3]

On the educational scene the picture was not all dark, however. At the 1930 convention of the Progressive Education Association, discussion revolved about the question

[3] Meyer, *op. cit.*, p. 424.

of how progressive education might be extended more effectively to the secondary level. The problem of college entrance requirements appeared to present a difficulty requiring study and recommendation. It was suggested that the executive board of the Progressive Education Association appoint a committee to explore the possibilities of better coordination of school and college work and to seek an agreement which would provide freedom for secondary schools to attempt fundamental reconstruction. The result was the establishment of the Commission on the Relation of School and College. Based on a one-year analysis of American high schools the commission proposed an experiment in which twenty public and private secondary schools would be invited to redesign their offerings with a view to achieving the following six objectives: (1) greater mastery in learning, (2) more continuity of learning, (3) the release of the creative energies of students, (4) a clearer understanding of the problems and of contemporary civilization, (5) better individual guidance of students, and (6) better teaching materials and more effective teaching.

There ensued the celebrated *Eight-Year Study* which ran from 1933 to 1941. Ultimately, thirty secondary schools participated in the project, and more than 300 colleges agreed to take part by waiving their formal admissions requirements for recommended graduates of these schools during the term of the experiment. Out of this experiment certain common reforms emerged. The standard subjects gained new vitality, and ancient barriers between departments were broken down as subject matter was reorganized around student interests. Indeed, many of the schools successfully influenced surrounding communities to develop similar programs. Furthermore, in final evaluations of college students drawn from graduates of one of the thirty participating secondary schools matched with graduates of other secondary schools, it was found that graduates of the participating secondary schools (1) earned a slightly higher total grade average, (2) received slightly more academic honors in each of the four years, and (3) seemed to possess a higher degree of intellectual curiosity and drive and, in addition to other positive attributes, appeared to have developed clearer ideas concerning the purposes of education.

Thus, in the face of generally adverse conditions, there was stimulating and, for the most part, productive activity in public education in the critical years between 1929 and 1938.

HIGHER EDUCATION IN AND AFTER THE DEPRESSION

The literature of the times indicates a period of some intellectual ferment. Educators and American education were subjected to several types of criticism. Part of the censure grew out of two serious studies of higher education; Abraham Flexner's comparative study of American, English and German universities (1930) and Robert Hutchins' *The Higher Learning in America* (1936). Both studies assailed the profusion, specialization, and chaos in the multitude of schools and courses prevailing in institutions of higher learning and, above all, the devotion to occupational and pecuniary interests. The charge was primarily against what appeared to these authors as disproportionate vocational emphases at the expense of the intellectual and cultural development of the college student. The discussions engendered by these works fanned the flame of an issue (never fully resolved) regarding relative values in higher education as, for example, the humanities versus scientific studies, the theoretical versus the practical emphasis, and the breadth versus the depth approach to learning. The multiplication of course offerings, the effects of the elective system, changes in the nature of the student population, and other conditions stimulated deliberation and action relative to the undergraduate programs of colleges and universities. Out of these deliberations there developed programs of what was commonly designated as "general education," the intent of which was to counteract the tendency toward premature specialization on the part of undergraduates and to lay the foundations of general culture. Such programs often entailed a series of integrated courses involving the humanities, the social sciences, and the natural sciences. By the mid-1940s such programs were fairly commonly adopted by colleges and undergraduate divisions of universities.

Teacher education, as well as general college and university education, came under serious examination in the years between the two world wars. In 1930 the *National Survey of the Education of Teachers* was undertaken under the auspices of the National Education Association, with Dr. E. S. Evenden as director. This survey grew out of grave concern about teacher preparation which had been growing for several years. The completed report furnished extensive information on the status of teacher education in normal schools, teachers colleges, colleges, and universities. In 1935, in the *Twenty-third Yearbook of the National Society of College Teachers of Education*, the survey was criticized for not giving more attention to trends in elementary and secondary education as a basis for evaluating current progress in teacher preparation and as a source of constructive proposals. The gist of this criticism was that the purposes of teacher education had their starting point in the purposes of elementary and secondary education and that no real progress could be made in the former without extensive considerations of the latter. The Commission of Teacher Education, organized by the American Council on Education in 1938, was intended, in part, to carry on such study.

Throughout this period of ferment, there were persistent pressures for an expansion of the graduate program in education and for modifications of standards relative to graduate degrees. During the fourth decade of the twentieth century, teacher-training institutions were operating in a situation in which the demand for new teachers was less than the supply of professionally trained persons, and there was an added stimulation for improving their product.

Between the two world wars, three major social developments altered greatly the progress and organization of graduate work: tremendous increase in numbers and change in character of the graduate population; shift in production of research from almost complete concentration in the universities to government, endowed, and industrial or commercial agencies; and competition between public and private agencies for control of the results and procedures of research. In addition, professional schools of education were faced with the decision as to whether the traditional doctor of philosophy degree was the desirable or even suitable degree for their total clientele, especially since many educational leaders were more concerned with preparing graduate students for service to society than with maintaining traditional concepts of graduate study. In a report entitled *Graduate Study for Future College Teachers*, released by the American Council on Education Commission on College Teaching, the editor pointed up the significance of this issue in the following statement:

In our national effort, one hundred years ago, to bring American scholarship up to European standards, it was right to lay special emphasis upon training in research. But by so doing, the problems of teaching were neglected. This became increasingly apparent as our colleges expanded in numbers and drew into their student bodies people of diverse backgrounds and disparate abilities and preparations. . . . There should be established another doctor's degree, not less rigorous, but different.

The subject of the nature and function of graduate work engaged the attention of professional educators during this entire decade and well into the next.

SUMMARY

The decade 1929–39 was one of paradoxes no less than any previous decade. It shook the nation with calamitous events which overthrew much in the existing social order. These were years of disillusionment which witnessed serious threats to persons and programs in education as well as to the general welfare of the citizenry.

The economic and political upheaval affected business

and industry and particularly the degree of governmental control in socioeconomic affairs. References to moving in the direction of the welfare state were widespread in America for the first time in this period of turbulence. The government had never participated so directly in educational matters as it did during the great Depression. This involvement had positive connotations both for the educational opportunities afforded youth and adults and for the provision of gainful employment for many who otherwise might have found employment impossible.

The heightened sensitivities which resulted from the traumatic impact of the economic and social collapse may have contributed to the several searching inquiries to which education was subjected in the 1930s. Progressive educators conducted an eight-year experiment to extend the benefits of progressive education to the secondary level and to look for closer approachment between the high schools and the colleges. Any tendency to foster imbalance on the side of the purely technical or professional in the undergraduate curricula of the nation's colleges was offset by the introduction of the program of general or liberal education intended to provide a rich academic background in organized knowledge and human activities. Teacher education came under scrutiny through the "National Survey of the Education of Teachers," and, finally, the many-faceted issue of the place of graduate study in professional education became the subject of study and debate. For some of the questions raised, answers were found; others remain unresolved to the present day.

Between 1929 and 1938 educators faced severe and perplexing problems. They had to wrestle with curtailed finances and facilities while attempting to maintain the standards and the gains attained by public education. They also were presented with stimulating challenges to support forward movements to raise the quality of American education. In neither instance was it possible for leaders in education to remain phlegmatic or unresponsive. This situation obtained, no less, for the faculty and administration of the School of Education of New York University.

IMPACT OF THE DEPRESSION ON THE SCHOOL OF EDUCATION
Status of Aims and Purposes

While goals and purposes of the School of Education had been delineated in 1921 in terms of the extended functions contemplated by the institution, a constant vigilance relative to social and educational forces which might impinge on these aims was suggested in minutes of faculty meetings between 1930 and 1933. For example, in 1930 Dean Withers asked the faculty to give time and thought to three proposed projects pertinent to the underlying policy of the School. These were a study of the best thoughts of outstanding leaders in education, a study of contemporary thinking on the part of leaders in fields other than education, and a study of the philosophies and programs of progressive institutions.

At a meeting of the faculty held on March 14, 1932 the major portion of the discussion revolved about the policy of the teacher-education unit of the University in the light of current trends. Among the topics considered were unemployment, the status of teachers in New York City, and the responsibility of education in relation to other social institutions. The dean urged full participation in these considerations and requested each member of the faculty to submit individual statements of position and recommendation with respect to the various issues.

Again, in January, 1933, the faculty heard the dean discuss a plan for faculty presentations of various phases of the philosophy and procedures of the School of Education. At that time he invited suggestions of additional topics for future discussions.

The seriousness with which the dean approached the matter of policy in these critical times is conveyed in the following statements:

Dean Withers mentioned certain factors which must be considered in deciding upon future policy, such as: (1) a determination of our real philosophy of education, a philosophy which must be attuned to the times in which we live; (2) a study of the trends in the development of other schools, and (3) a study of fields not now adequately serviced to determine what contributions our School can make in these newer fields.

Regrettably, the record fails to provide further information with regard to the issues and topics under discussion or to specific ways in which the philosophy of the School of Education was modified—if it was—during the remaining years of the Withers administration. Changing concepts, therefore, must be adduced from subsequent actions which reflected change in policy and modifications in structure and program.

Facilities

Although the twelve-story building, dedicated on February 28, 1930, was designed to be but one unit of an education block of buildings, funds did not permit the erection of the remaining sections, nor have such sections been added to this day.

However, the new building provided modern facilities for the Departments of Physical Education, Music Education, Home Economics, Art Education, and Vocational Education. It also made other improvements in facilities possible. For example, except for office space, the work of the Department of Music Education was moved to the new building, and the former premises of the department at 80 Washington Square East were henceforth designated as the Students Building. A School of Education student council was established and a program of student activities, with a faculty director, was inaugurated. In addition, with expanded facilities in the new building, the Department of Physical Education and Health instituted a health service for students and faculty. Laboratory and clinical rooms were set up in two areas: the Psycho-Education Clinic in the Department of Educational Psychology and the Clinic for the Gifted in the Department of Educational Sociology. The building made available an auditorium seating about 500 for productions of the Dramatic Art Department and for other student and professional meetings. The easing of space in the School's original quarters made possible establishment of a statistical laboratory containing various computing and other mechanical aids. This laboratory was operated under the Department of Administration and Supervision and was opened in 1932.

In 1936 the central University administration assumed the debt on the total properties. Loans were secured through local banks, and the outstanding bonds were called for redemption. By common agreement among the officers of the Realty Corporation, the officers of administration of the School of Education, and the central University administration, the School of Education Realty Corporation was dissolved in 1937.

In the fall of 1937, Dr. Edgar Starr Barney, principal of the Hebrew Technical Institute, placed before Assistant Dean Ralph E. Pickett the question of whether New York University would be interested in taking over the work of the institute. Dean Pickett brought the question before Dean Withers and Assistant Dean Payne and they agreed that the School of Education would not want to operate the institue as such but that there would be a great interest in trying to work out an arrangement whereby the buildings and equipment might be used for the industrial arts and vocational education activities of the School of Education. At that time the shops for these activities were scattered in the basement of the building known as the Press Annex, the first floor of the South Building, and the eleventh floor of the new Education Building. The crowding was so bad and the lack of adequate facilities so great, that the opportunity to get the Institute space and facilities was exceedingly attractive.

Dean Withers obtained approval from the chancellor to explore possibilities. Professor Badger and Mr. Lawrence Payson were the representatives of the central administration in the protracted negotiations that ensued. Increasingly, Withers turned over to Assistant Dean Payne the responsibilities of the office of dean in these negotiations, inasmuch as it became apparent that the negotiations would not be completed before his retirement. Assistant

Dean Pickett, together with Professor William P. Sears, Jr., handled the negotiations in the interests of the Department of Vocational Education. The actual transfer of location and the first functioning under the new lease took place in 1939 after E. George Payne had succeeded John W. Withers as dean of the School of Education.[4]

Finally, during the first year of the economic collapse in the nation, the School of Education established a Bureau of Educational Placement and Services, the first effort in the direction of such a service to students and alumni within the University.

Despite these gains in physical facilities and services, Withers commented on the continuing need for more and better facilities in student housing, for a dean of women, and for improved library facilities.

Staff

Sixty-three persons were added to the instructional staff between 1929 and 1938. From the data of Table VI, page 168, it will be observed that the largest increase both in full professorships and in total staff occurred between the academic years 1929–30 and 1930–31. The sharp drop in total personnel in 1931–32 involved individuals from the ranks of instructor and part-time lecturer. Aside from this drop and a slight fluctuation between 1932 and 1934 the trend was upward throughout this period. This is more clearly apparent when presented graphically in Figure 2, page 170, based on data from Table VI.

[4] *Memorandum* from Ralph E. Pickett to Miss Elsie Hug, dated August 5, 1963.

TABLE VI

NUMBER AND DISTRIBUTION OF FACULTY PERSONNEL
SCHOOL OF EDUCATION
1929–38

Year	Profs.	Assoc. Profs.	Asst. Profs.	Instrs.	Lects.	Total
1929–30	22	9	15	58	28	132
1930–31	32	15	12	69	45	173
1931–32	32	16	15	59	26	148
1932–33	35	13	18	64	22	152
1933–34	33	12	19	68	16	148
1934–35	34	10	19	69	28	160
1935–36	35	16	18	69	22	160
1936–37	34	14	17	87	24	176
1937–38	33	15	22	75	50	195
1938–39	37	12	22	76	72	219

Among those joining the faculty in this decade were:

1929   Samuel L. Hamilton headed the newly constituted Department of Religious Education.

1930   Albert B. Meredith succeeded the dean as chairman of the Department of Administration and Supervision. Dr. Meredith came to the University from the commissionership of education in the state of Connecticut although he had taught courses in administration in the School of Pedagogy in 1918.

Robert K. Speer assumed the chairmanship of the Department of Elementary Education, having come from Teachers College, Columbia University.

Rollin H. Tanner, former Professor of Classics in the University College of Arts and Science, was brought from University Heights to head the newly established Department of Foreign Languages and Literature.

1935   Randolf Somerville, who directed the work in Dramatic Art in Washington Square College and who had been instrumental in forming the original Washington Square Players, also assumed responsi-

bility for the Department of Dramatic Art set up
in the School of Education in this year.

Two other areas set up at this time under departmental
structure were: 1932, Supervised Student Teaching
(changed to Coordination of Teacher Training in 1935).
Responsibilities here were divided between Frithiof C.
Borgeson, who handled the work at the elementary level,
and Arthur D. Whitman, who was in charge of such duties
at the secondary level. In 1935 certain courses were
grouped under the heading General Education, with no
assigned administrative head. This designation was
changed to nondepartmental in 1937.

From the graphic presentation of figure 2, page 000, it
is apparent that the situation with respect to staff in the
School of Education showed remarkably little setback in
this era. Although the teaching load during this period
was changed from twelve to fifteen hours for full-time
faculty members, faculty salaries were not cut at any time
during the Depression, nor were increments entirely un-
known in this decade. Once again the dean expressed the
wish that the spirit of cooperation so typical of the faculty
in the past would continue to characterize the faculty in
the years to come.

Student Body

While an examination of Table VII, page 171, reveals
a steady increase in graduate enrollment between 1929 and
1938, the undergraduates remained the larger student
body. The distribution with respect to the sexes was much
more closely matched in the graduate group, with differences ranging from less than 100 to a maximum of 200

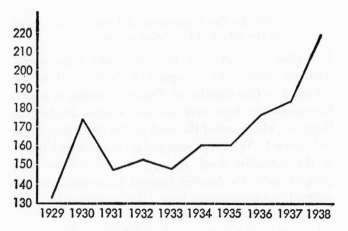

Fig. 2 – Distribution – Total Faculty Personnel
School of Education 1929-38

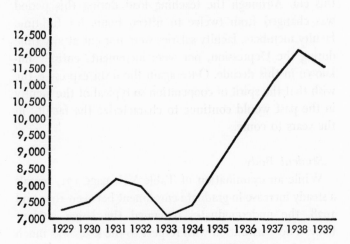

Fig. 3 Enrollment Distribution
School of Education 1929-39

TABLE VII

ENROLLMENT DISTRIBUTION — SCHOOL OF EDUCATION
1929-39

Year	Undergraduate			Graduate			Totals		
	Men	Women	Total	Men	Women	Total	Men	Women	Totals
1929-30	1620	4399	6019	626	589	1215	2246	4988	7234
1930-31	1858	4091	5949	715	829	1544	2573	4920	7493
1931-32	1963	3968	5931	1221	1117	2338	3184	5085	8269
1932-33	1940	3660	5600	1211	1132	2343	3151	4792	7943
1933-34	1651	3112	4763	1170	1106	2276	2821	4218	7039
1934-35	1612	2982	4594	1383	1378	2761	2995	4360	7355
1935-36	1629	3651	5280	1621	1870	3491	3250	5521	8771
1936-37	1672	4070	5742	2002	2152	4154	3674	6222	9896
1937-38	1751	4622	6373	2342	2559	4901	4093	7181	11,274
1938-39	1853	5019	6872	2556	2655	5211	4409	7674	12,083

apparent in the entire distribution. Where such differences do occur, they are in favor of the male group. From the undergraduate figures it may be seen that the females always outnumber the males by a considerable margin. Nevertheless, totals for the decade present the amazing picture of a 41 percent increase in enrollment during the most drastic economic period in the nation's history. From a total enrollment of 4984 immediately preceding the Depression, the figure rose to 12,083 by 1938–39.

The record indicates that financial assistance was available to students from several sources. One of these was from within the University as implied in the following statements from the minutes of a general committee meeting held in December, 1930:

> Dean Withers read to the faculty a communication from Mr. Voorhis, (Secretary of the University), covering procedures to be adopted in helping to meet the general employment situation. . . . It was suggested that whatever recommendations the Dean may make to Mr. Voorhis, he will take into consideration the fact that relatively limited funds of the faculty should be so used as to enable help to be given first to needy students in the School of Education.

A second type of tuition relief came through such governmental agencies as the National Youth Administration and the Federal Economic Recovery Administration. Students partially amortized these obligations in a variety of ways. For example, in commenting on the work of the Department of Physical Education and Health, the dean pointed out that at the undergraduate level many students rendered service in connection with the Public Works Division, the Civil Works Administration, the Federal Economic Recovery Administration, and other governmental agencies. He stated that:

From twelve to fifteen of the boys have been placed as educational directors in the CCC camps; a number with the educational division of the Indian Service, and many others with semi-private and public agencies. Requests for part-time work of graduate students who are pursuing their courses with us are increasing. Churches, settlement houses, boys clubs, and other community agencies are looking to the Department for part-time help.

The dean noted further that the psycho-educational clinic "rendered splendid service during the year." In so doing, it furnished excellent practice for the graduate students specializing in this field. An interesting commentary on the impact of the times may be seen in the dean's revelation that "there has been also during the year an unusual demand made by students for conferences in connection with their own personality difficulties."

Probably the greatest impact of the Depression on the enrollment was on the proportion of students coming from a distance as compared with the enrollment from the New York City environs, the latter group constituting 60 percent of the total. Thus, these years imposed another frustration on the institution's aim to serve a population of wider geographic distribution than the local and metropolitan.

The area in which the School of Education manifested the greatest activity during this turbulent decade was in its expanded and reorganized program.

The Program

Signs of curtailment and retrenchment, generally characteristic of the Depression, were not visible in the instructional program of the School of Education.

Between 1929 and 1938, six new departments or areas

of study were added. These were foreign languages and literature, adult education, religious education, (reconstituted) dramatic art, supervised student teaching (later called coordination of teacher training), and general education (subsequently designated as nondepartmental courses). Immediate response to the spirit of the times is discernible in at least the first two of these.

While the Depression played havoc with education in general, this was not the case in the realm of adult learning. There was an appreciable rise in the national appetite for such learning and an impressive augmentation in the arrangements made to cope with it. Following grants by the federal government, there appeared in the nation at large thousands of classes for more than 1,500,000 adults manned by more than 40,000 otherwise unemployed teachers. School of Education sensitivity to this national movement was reflected in the establishment of a Department of Adult Education in 1935. The dean supervised the work of this department. In the second instance, the incorporation of a group of cultural courses under the designation General Education suggests another example where the teacher-education unit of New York University took an early lead in a movement which was only in its infancy in the decade under discussion, as indicated on page 159.

Expansion of listings occurred in fourteen departments; eight others showed erratic listings, but with no loss of courses below the figure shown for 1929; five departments, which had remained relatively stable in the previous decade, continued to do so throughout the 1930s, and only one department reduced its offerings by fifty percent during the depression years. These distributions are shown in the tabulation below:

Increased Offerings

Art Education	Home Economics
Business Education	Physical Education
Educational Psychology	Science Education
Educational Sociology	Social Studies
English Education	Adult Education
Dramatic Art	General Education
Foreign Language and Literature	Vocational Education

Reduced Offerings

Philosophy of Education

Remained Static

Creative Education
Expiremental Education
History of Education
Mathematics Education
Student Teaching

Erratic

Administration-Supervision
College Education
Elementary Education
Music Education
Personnel Administration
Religious Education
Secondary Education
Teachers College
Normal School Education

Between 1929 and 1939 the number of departments increased from 23 to 28. Total course offerings show a gain of 65 percent, rising from 555 in 1929 to 850 in 1938. The

titles of selected courses under the Nondepartmental offerings, and introduced in this period, reflect types of issues
which were receiving academic attention in these critical
times. Such titles included:

1] *Our Times in the News*
2] *The Schools and Their Critics*
   Personal and Financial
   Problems of the Teacher
   Educating for Safety
   The Motion Picture: Its
        Artistic, Social Aspects
   Women in the Professions
   Radio in the Classroom
   Character Development in a Democracy
3] *Public Opinion and Education*
   Educ. for Social Reconstruction

The courses numbered (1), (2), and (3) were concerned
with the issues, referred to on page 154, relating to possible un-American activities on the part of some teachers
and the relationship to academic freedom. In 1936 the
chancellor wrote:

The situation with regard to the preservation of proper
academic freedom seems less acute than a year ago. Not that
attacks on its exercise do not still continue. They do, and
will. However, the systematic drive to implant in the public
mind the idea that teaching should be regarded as a suspect
profession seems to have passed its high-water mark.

In a year of great national distress, Withers wrote: "In
many respects the year has been an exciting one, involving
new undertakings and many new problems."

Among the new undertakings may be mentioned the work in aeronautics education for the training of aviation groundschool teachers. During 1930-31, seventy-two persons sought training in this area through courses offered in the School of Education and sponsored by the Daniel Guggenheim Fund Committee on Elementary and Secondary Aeronautics Education. The director of this work, Roland H. Spaulding, in cooperation with the army air corps and the federal board of vocational education, prepared a training manual for use in the army as well as in commercial aircraft corporations.

In conjunction with the inauguration of the School of Education's Department of Foreign Languages and Literatures, there was transferred from Columbia University a service bureau for classical teachers established by the American Classical League to assist Latin teachers throughout the United States.

The use of audiovisual aids was brought into the teaching techniques taught in the Department of the Social Studies, and this department, through the Institute of Education, offered courses at the New York City Museum of Natural History.

In commenting upon the discipline of educational sociology, Withers pointed out that recent years had witnessed increasing emphasis upon use of scientific techniques in the study of human relations in general, and sociology in particular had made distinct contributions to research in these important fields. He noted that in sociology the movement seemed to be definitely away from the philosophical emphasis so characteristic of the past and in the direction of more scientific research. With regard to the latter, the Department of Educational Sociology sponsored three research projects during 1931–32. There were:

1] a study in social background and community organization,

2] studies of the adjustment of the individual to social life with implications for education, and

3] studies in various aspects of public health in their sociological and educational significances.

To encourage the wider distribution of results of research in this area, under the leadership of the chairman of the department, Dr. E. George Payne, the members of the department launched the *Journal of Educational Sociology*. In addition, the department worked out a cooperative relationship with the New York School for Social Work which led to incorporation of a new program of study for the preparation of social caseworkers. In 1936 Payne listed the following significant activities of the Department:

1] formation of an Educational Sociology Club, with emphasis on recognition of various cultural groups;

2] participation of Professors Thrasher and Zorbaugh in a conference on crime prevention;

3] conduct of the Boys Club Study (with special reference to crime and juvenile delinquency); and

4] participation to provide and permit social control of motion pictures shown to children.

The record for this period contains evidence that distinct changes were made in the organization of city schools, in the treatment of the curriculum, and in individual school and classroom procedures as a result of the work of Mearns in Creative Education, a field which continued to receive much publicity from the press and radio all through the 1930s.

Interest in that facet of progressive education referred to as the activity program was at its height in these years, and training in this technique was included in the work of the Department of Secondary Education as well as in the Department of Elementary Education. The earliest proponents of this concept of teaching held that learning takes place in the response, and consequently what is important is, not the gathering and storing of facts, but their use and application. Along with other components of progressive education, the principles of the activity program came under scutiny in such studies as: J. Wayne Wrightstone's *Appraisal of Newer Elementary School Practices,* J. Cayce Morrison's *The Activity Program* (1935–40), and *The Eight-Year Study* (see p. 157).

The staff of the Department of Secondary Education also undertook publication of *The Junior-Senior Clearing House,* classed as the best journal published in the national high school field.

The dean submitted, as evidence of the quality of work done in the Department of Art Education, the fact that of the twenty-one individuals who had passed the license examinations for teachers of art in 1931, thirteen were graduates of the department at the School of Education.

A publicity release issued by the New York University Bureau of Public Information and dated September 23, 1936, makes reference to a unique, but short-lived experiment by the Department of College Education to extend formal training for teachers in professional schools. The release read, in part:

New York University inaugurated last night a new group of courses in dental education designed to make instruction more effective to the dental student and to society. The new program, offered by the University's School of Education in cooperation with the College of Dentistry, makes the University the first institution of its kind in the United States to provide formal training for dental teachers leading toward higher degrees.

Finally, under the leadership of A. B. Meredith, the Department of Administration and Supervision conducted four school surveys between 1931 and 1933.

This array of activities, undertaken in connection with the programs of the various departments of the School of Education in a decade generally characterized by retrenchment, implies a continuation of the vitality which had made itself felt soon after the reorganization of the teacher-education division of the University. While proliferation and duplication continued to be apparent, both in the instances previously discussed and in at least one other area, it would appear that the administration was not entirely unaware of this fact; in at least one instance the dean acknowledged awareness of the situation. In discussing the expanded work of the Department of the Social Studies he stated:

The fields of economics, government, geography, and history are closely related to those of psychology and sociology, but these disciplines are organized as separate departments in the School of Education. These fields have many problems in common and there are certain duplications in the work, some of which could be eliminated by careful study of the content of the courses offered.

As departments envisioned broader opportunities for service, an increasing number of non-teaching programs was added which included the following:

Department	Program Added
Administration and Supervision	Comptrollers, Directors of Finance, Directors of Public Relations, Registrars and Recorders, Directors of Reference, and Research Supervisors and Administrators for all educational levels
College Education	College Presidents Deans of Administration Deans of Instruction
Educational Psychology	School Psychologists
Educational Sociology	Workers and Administrators in various community Agencies including Social Case Workers
Guidance and Personnel Adminis.	Personnel and Placement Officers Educational Counselors
Home Economics Education	Hospital Dieticians
Music Education	Directors of Instrumental Music, Choral Conductors
Physical Education and Health	Health Supervisors and Co-ordinators Directors and Supervisors of Public Health Nursing Directors and Supervisors of Institutional Nursing
Religious Education	Directors and Supervisors of Religious Education Home and Overseas Missionaries

This was in keeping with the new role assumed by the School of Education in 1921, looking toward the preparation of men and women for all types of educational and community services. Thus, there was an identifiable effort on the part of the faculty and administration of the institution to carry out its stated aims and objectives.

Reorganizaion of Graduate Work

In a decade of intensive and varied activity, there was no phase of the institution's academic responsibilities which received greater attention than did the status and future development of its graduate work. Once again, the issues which arose had a long history of concern behind them.

In 1905 the complaint had been made that it was becoming increasingly unrealistic to base an appointment of any grade higher than instructor on teaching record alone. Three years later Flexner deplored the fact that universities had sacrificed college teaching at the altar of research.

In 1908 Horne, of New York University's School of Pedagogy, reported the results of a questionnaire addressed to presidents of colleges and universities in New England inquiring into their attitudes toward work in education for prospective college teachers. The vote, as usual, was split; eleven were favorable, and the other seven exhibited various attitudes of non-encouragement.

Lowell, of Harvard, in 1909 spoke of the "monstrous number" attending graduate schools, and by 1916 West, of Princeton, was worried about "the most sordid and dangerous thing just now in our graduate schools; namely, that they are attracting men, not because they must be scholars, but because they want a job." "Why," the dean asked, "is the degree made the be-all and end-all? It is beginning to be known like a union card for labor."

Perhaps the recurrent character of the arguments regarding graduate study can best be summarized by the frequent pleas for someone to settle the question of what the doctorate was *for*. The question came up with alarming regularity in each decade and no clear-cut final answer appears to have emerged to date. When in 1922 Harvard decided to give the doctorate for work in education but to give it the designation "doctor of education," another subject for endless debate was introduced.

It is little wonder that by 1930 the administration and faculty of the School of Education were impelled to reassess the roles of graduate degrees in this professional school. Early in 1930 Withers requested A. B. Meredith, recently appointed chairman of the Department of Administration and Supervision, to accept the chairmanship of the Committee on Admissions and Student Standing—Graduate Wing and to undertake, through the committee and any necessary subcommittees, the complete reappraisal of graduate study in the School of Education, and to bring recommendations to the faculty for action.

Some of the proposals emanating from faculty deliberations failed of fruition, and some were adopted and led to further growth. Among the former was a plan to divide the School of Education into three divisions: a junior college, a senior college, and a graduate school. In presenting such a recommendation to the chancellor, the dean pointed out that the chief purpose of the proposal was to make possible serious study by the faculty of certain problems of junior college education arising out of the general disposition:

1] to establish junior colleges throughout the United States,

2] to regard the junior college as an essential part of the American system of public education,

3] to admit to such colleges qualified high school graduates without regard to their occupational purpose or their place in society,

4] to expect the faculties of such institutions to render to these students instruction and guidance adjusted to their peculiar needs and capacities, and

5] to determine curricula organization and methods of instruction best suited for this purpose.

If approved, the plan contemplated admission of students to the junior college unit with provision of instruction needed to prepare them for the senior division and to admit qualified graduates of high schools still undecided on their future occupation or on whether they wished to embark upon four years of college training in arts and sciences.

While a subcommittee of the faculty continued to study the above proposal and make further recommendations, neither the full faculty nor the chancellor evidenced strong interest or encouragement in the project, and the proposal for this form of academic organization was never presented to the faculty for formal action.

On the other hand, the first change relating to graduate study approved by the faculty represented a modification in basic philosophy. This called for acceptance of school-wide responsibility for the conduct and quality of doctoral work. The implementation of this philosophy required several procedural changes. Where previously the doctoral applicant had submitted to four written examinations in educational psychology, educational sociology, history of education, and philosophy of education, demonstration of competency in these areas was moved to the master's level. It was now proposed to administer for admission to doctoral candidacy, a general written examination intended to assess aptitude and to measure potential capacity to do doctoral work, especially with reference to those disciplines required in research. The selection of the doctoral candidate was transferred from the decision of an individual faculty member to a faculty committee established for this purpose. The oral interview, previously conducted by the dean, the faculty member from the area of specialization sought, and representatives from the four disciplines named above, was abandoned.

Another change was establishment of the sponsoring committee system. This called for the appointment of a committee of three members of the full-time faculty holding the rank of assistant professor, associate professor, or full professor. The selection of the chairman of this sponsoring committee was the student's prerogative, subject to the acceptance by the designated professor. Among the duties of the sponsoring committee were (1) determination and approval of the candidate's selection of courses, (2) assistance in the preparation of an outline of proposed research, and (3) guidance in the development and the writing of the dissertation.

A third innovation was the introduction of a Subcommittee on Higher Degrees for the review and approval of the outline of proposed research. The subcommittee was charged with the responsibility for guarding the quality of research and of maintaining uniform standards.

A final written integration examination was added to come toward the end of the program and to serve as a measure of the synthesis of the candidate's experience gained through his course of study.

The final requirement was an oral examination conducted by a commission consisting of the individual's sponsoring committee and two additional members of the faculty. A defense of the dissertation was the major purpose of this test. With some modification in the title and function of the outlines committee and with revisions of the qualifying examination, the plan, formally adopted on November 18, 1935, has continued to operate to the present.

In consonance with another trend in American higher education, the faculty committees in the School of Education studying the graduate programs included in their deliberations consideration of the doctor of education as a second professional degree to be conferred by New York University through the School of Education. It was becoming increasingly clear to the faculty that the diversity in backgrounds and professional objectives apparent in doctoral applicants required two distinct doctors' degrees in order to construct programs and permit the range of research appropriate for these several objectives.

In America the doctor of education degree had both proponents and opponents. Its detractors asserted it was a cheap degree provided in response to pressure from professional people who were not interested in undergoing the rigors under which the doctor of philosophy degree was gestated and delivered. On the other side, it was held that the philosophy degree served primarily to prepare individuals merely to do research and under conditions that the professional man could not easily duplicate after leaving the graduate campus. Research under laboratory conditions, it was suggested, had little transfer value in practical situations.

The long sessions over whether the requirement in foreign languages should be reserved exclusively to the doctor of philosophy candidate, and what should be the distinguishing characteristics of the research for the two degrees were not restricted to the faculty of the School of Education. Rather they were symptomatic of the recorded confusion among graduate departments and schools of education regarding their most important functions. The variety of demands made upon them and the lack of criteria for determining the proper uses of their resources led to a distraction which resulted in some loss of efficiency and effectiveness.

The distinction generally accepted between the doctor of education and the doctor of philosophy in education was that suggested by the terms professional training and research.

The faculty of the School of Education, although accepting in principle this broad distinction, found considerable difficulty in arriving at fixed and clear-cut lines of demarcation to distinguish between identifiable areas of research for the two degrees. By 1934, the year in which the Council of the University authorized the School of Education to recommend candidates for the doctor of education degree, the faculty had approved, in terms of broad guide lines, the two statements following:

Ph.D. represents in its thesis a useful, scientific, and acceptable contribution to education theory.

Ed.D. represents in its final document an immediately useful contribution to education practice.

In spite of these two statements, questions of interpretation continued (and continue) to arise. One assumption which might be made regarding this fluidity of distinction between research areas is that it is indicative of a dynamic approach to educational research. This in turn may be considered to be a healthy state because it opens the future to greater creativity in intellectual inquiry rather than too closely circumscribing avenues of possible development.

Following announcement of authorization to accept candidates for the doctor of education degree, Horne wrote to the dean as follows:

"First, congratulations again on securing for the School of Education the privilege of conferring the Ed.D. degree without losing the Ph.D. Really it was necessary for our survival." [5]

Horne went on to state that the distinction between the two degrees should be that between practice and theory, the one being for sucessful experience and achievement and the other for scientific research and contribution to knowledge. This was in accord with the position generally taken by the faculty. The structural plan set up for the doctor of philosophy degree, including a preliminary examination, appointment of a sponsoring committee, and submission of an outline of proposed research, was made

[5] *Letter* from Herman H. Horne to John W. Withers, dated June 14, 1934.

operative for the doctor of education degree with two modifications: (1) the preliminary examination for the doctor of education candidates placed greater emphasis on demonstrated knowledge in the field of education; (2) the foreign language requirement was omitted for the doctor of education degree, but two foundations courses were required instead. These were *Problems of Contemporary Life* and *Education as a State Function.*

Within the first five years following inauguration of the doctor of education degree in 1934, sixty-four such degrees were awarded. On the other hand, within the same period 157 doctor of philosophy degrees were earned. The ratio leveled off to practically even distribution until the period following World War II when, once again the traditional doctor of philosophy degree was in the ascendency. The award of such a sizable number of education doctorates in the five-year span indicates two things: (1) about one third of the number were candidates who transferred from the doctor of philosophy to the doctor of education degree; (2) the other two thirds did not procastinate in the completion of their degree requirements.

Adoption of the new plan for doctors' degrees imposed additional responsibilities and functions on members of the full-time faculty, for which no recognition in the form of compensation or released time was given. However, with this tightening of the policy and design of work at the doctoral level, the faculty hoped to raise the quality of work and of the ultimate product for the doctorate, thereby safeguarding the integrity of the degrees while making them more meaningful for the candidate in a professional school.

During this period efforts were begun to revise and improve the program for the master's degree as one of the major functions of the program. Formal actions effecting changes at this level did not come until the next decade, under the leadership of Withers' successor.

By 1938–39 the graduate group represented 43.1 percent of the total enrollment in the School of Education (*see* Table VII, page 171).

Resumé of Program

Through its growth in course offerings from 555 in 1929 to 850 in 1938, the School of Education maintained its policy of extending and pioneering in professional education. Pioneering efforts are seen in the inclusion of courses directly related to the public welfare such as those concerned with crime prevention, juvenile delinquency, and the influence of the motion picture. Community services were increased through the work of the Departments of Educational Psychology and Educational Sociology and by establishment of the Psycho-Education Clinic, and the Clinic for the Gifted. The incorporation of a program of general education and adult education were direct responses to contemporary educational movements. The Department of Foreign Languages and Literatures which was incorporated into the total program in this decade, together with the enriched offerings in elementary and secondary education, gave evidence of alertness to curricular changes taking place at these levels.

The faculty and administration of the teacher-education division revealed a sense of obligation to the profession when, as early as 1929, in discussing suitable subjects for master's and doctoral theses, it was maintained that where case titles involving subject matter were presented, these must reflect educational implications and applications in order that the researches might be properly sponsored by a member of the faculty of the School of Education. This respect for the quality of its graduate work was again demonstrated in concern for standards in the conduct of and admission to graduate seminars.

The graduate program as revised contained inherent strengths and weaknesses. For example, the professionalization of the doctor of philosophy degree and the inclusion of the doctor of education degree was an indication of the upgrading of education doctorates which came in response to a growing conviction that the nation was becoming increasingly urbanized and industrialized and that there were needs of a practical, professional, and vocational nature which the traditional graduate program and degree could not fill.

These changes, coming as they did in a period of economic caution (as referred to by the assistant dean in charge of the budget on several occasions during the Depression years), fostered the possible weaknesses of having graduates and undergraduates, even though these were seniors, enrolled in the same classes. In other words, there was no discernible distinction made between instruction for upper undergraduates, for master's, or for doctoral students. Further, it is possible that the excessive cross-referencing of courses among several departments, which was the practice at this time, had an adverse effect on the breadth and depth of specialization as well as contributing to undue duplication.

Willingness to venture into what might seem to be unorthodox areas in a professional school, especially in times of economic stress, may be observed in the establishment of formal Departments of Religious Education and Dramatic Art and in the experiment to extend formal preparation for teachers in all professional schools.

The astounding growth in enrollment from 4984 students in 1928 to 12,083 in 1938 in part made possible the expansion of the School's program and had relevance to the growing influence of the School of Education in the field of professional education.

However, in a final accounting of the faculty activities relating to academic affairs between 1929 and 1938, the evidence would seem to support the conclusion that the decade ended with a credit balance. The program of the teacher-education unit of New York University provided for continued progress in the theory and practice of education at all levels and for extended service to the profession and the community.

SUMMARY

While the record indicates alertness on the part of the administration of the School of Education to the possible influence of an atypical cultural epoch on the policy of the institution, no formal actions taken during this period led to revision of the stated aims and purposes which appeared in the annual bulletins of the School between 1929 and 1938.

The opening of the twelve-story Education Building in 1930 led to improvements in the work of five departments—Art Education, Home Economics, Music Education, Physical Education, and Vocational Education—and permitted release of the space previously allotted to the Music Education Department for use as a Students Building. This, in turn, made possible establishment of a student council with a faculty adviser and the inauguration of a program of student activities.

A faculty health service, a well-equipped statistical laboratory, and a clinic for gifted children as well as one for children with emotional problems were feasible because of the facilities of the new building. Finally, space to house the Classical Teachers Bureau and the Bureau of Educational Placement and Services permitted increased assistance to students and alumni.

The general financial condition of the nation in the critical years of the Depression did not deter the institution from extending the available range of professional preparations nor from enlarging its staff in order to do so.

The School of Education extended the horizons of professional education in this decade by adapting its various curricula to the trends in theory and practice of education at all levels. Through surveys and other researches conducted in these years the School of Education continued to render professional services to public education and to other community agencies.

Midway in the last decade of his administration, Withers noted as among the more pressing and important needs in the maintenance and further development of the School of Education the following:

1] enlargement of the faculty to permit more effective and satisfactory service,

2] dormitory service at or near Washington Square for the increasing number of full-time students,

3] Improved facilities for instruction and research,

4] Erection, as soon as possible, of another building on the remaining property,

5] larger annual appropriations for the purchase of books and other materials of instruction,

6] better and more expanded library service for students and faculty,

7] more convenient and satisfactory office space for faculty and clerical staff and also seminar rooms of adequate size and equipment for conferences with graduate students,

8] better laboratory facilities, under the control of the School of Education, for supervised practice teaching at all levels and for the experimental and cooperative study of education,

9] fuller and more wholehearted cooperation between the faculty of the School of Education and those of other divisions of the University,

10] larger sums of money to be made available for three purposes: first, for types of educational research and the prosecution of studies already under way and of others that should be immediately started; second, for the endowment of fellowships and scholarships for the undergraduate and graduate students of demonstrated outstanding ability; third, for the establishment of a student loan fund, and

11] finally, that permission be granted as soon as possible to the administration of the School of Education to use its entire receipts from student fees for the improvement of its services to its own students.

A determination of the extent to which any or all of these suggestions were implemented will require a study of the School of Education in a subsequent era.

On April 6, 1938, not quite a half year before his retirement on August 31, 1938, Dean Withers submitted for the consideration of Chancellor Chase, the following recommendations:

1] In order to permit ample time for the selection of a successor, if no decision has been reached by the opening of the academic year 1938–39, appoint Assistant Dean E. George Payne as Acting Dean. If at the end of the year, this has proved satisfactory to all, appoint Payne to the Deanship of the School of Education.

2] Give consideration to replacement of top faculty members approaching age 65 who will be hard to replace. (As indirectly related to this, the Dean noted that in the past seventeen years the School of Education had awarded 498 Doctor's degrees, 3,657 Master's degrees, and 7,613 Bachelor's degrees).

3] Give assistance to Assistant Dean Pickett by appointing a new head of the Vocational Education Department; appoint an acting chairman of the Department of Educational Sociology in order to relieve Assistant Dean Payne, then chairman of the department.

4] Maintain the present policy of the School of Education. This policy and the underlying reasons for its adoption should be made perfectly clear to the faculty, students, and alumni of the School of Education. It should also be wholly understood and approved by the University administration.

5] The services which the School of Education strives to render should be made clear to schools and systems, both public and private, throughout the United States.

As a last point in his memorandum, the dean assured the chancellor of his sincere and earnest wish to continue to serve the School of Education and the University.

No response to this memorandum was found, and once again, the record of any actions growing out of it would come within the purview of another study.

6 · At the Half Century Mark

The Period

It was the best of times, it was the worst of times, it was the age of wisdom, it was the age of foolishness, . . . it was the epoch of Light, it was the season of Darkness. . . .

With these lines from A *Tale of Two Cities*, Dickens states they are as descriptive of the era in which he was writing as they were of the period of the French Revolution with which his story is concerned. They might well have been intended for the fifty years covering the first half century of teacher education at New York University.

In the year in which the first teacher-training unit at the university level opened as the School of Pedagogy of the University of the City of New York—1890 following two years of experimental efforts—the nation was reaping the full flush of the expansion which followed the end of the Civil War. This expansion was manifested in population growth, inventive genius, rapid accumulation of wealth, growing world power, and—fundamental to it all—an educational system indigenous to a democratic society. In 1938, the terminal year of this period, one nation stood on the brink of a darkness so savage as to shock the entire world. Between 1890 and 1938 the human condition passed through succeeding epochs of panic and prosperity, of social apathy and awakened social conscience, of inactivity and of change—in other words—through history.

The Educational Picture

In education the nation passed from a philosophy of limited support for education, primarily at the elementary level, to one of publicly supported education at all levels with efforts toward equal opportunity for all citizens. The processes of education moved from a regimented rigidity based largely on the German system of education to a permissiveness deplored by some educators as an abuse of the best tenets of progressive education. The swing of the pendulum from emphasis on the classic, traditional college curriculum to emphasis on the expedient and utilitarian studies created enduring problems and conflicts for educators as well as for those to be educated.

Education as a social institution met the challenges of succeeding decades with varying degrees of initiative and response. One of the responses was a continuing concern for the quality of instruction. From modest beginnings often representing little advance beyond secondary school education, the art of teaching and the science of education moved forward to the point at which teacher training was ready to assume the status of a discipline at the university level. The first example of this movement was the establishment of the School of Pedagogy of the University of the City of New York on March 3, 1890.

The School of Pedagogy

Although hampered by diversification in the backgrounds of its faculty as well as in its student body, the pioneering venture in graduate pedagogy did make contributions to the improvement of teacher qualifications by utilizing, in its instructional programs, the findings of the scientific movement in education which came toward the latter part of the nineteenth century and included the work of William James, Edward L. Thorndike, John Dewey, G. Stanley Hall, and the men who followed them in the development of the behavioral sciences. It further demonstrated leadership by introducing fields of study new to teacher-training programs, such as administration, art, music, and domestic science, even though the continued inclusion of these subjects in the program was subject to budgetary, enrollment, and other influences. Response to the trends in secondary education was discernible in the addition of work for the development of skills in commercial and industrial arts subjects.

The major orientation of most members of the faculty of the School of Pedagogy represented the classical tradition and forced the administration to look outside its own walls for instructors in these newer areas. The financial drain imposed by this necessity, together with loss of income due to free pedagogy courses available to New York City teachers, took a serious toll of the institution's resources. The further effect on enrollment of the first world war made it clear that a total reorganization was needed if the teacher-training division of New York University was to survive.

The School of Education

Within the half century under discussion professional education emerged as a distinct educational area. When teacher-preparing institutions moved from a concept of *training* to one of *education,* teaching became only one of the facets of professional service for which professional education provided preparation. Thus, the extension of the horizons of professional education was the significant difference between the School of Pedagogy and the new School of Education, so named in 1921.

Besides the change in name of the institution, additional recommendations for change, approved within the first year of the new administration, resulted in (1) an expanded statement of aims and purposes and (2) a reorganized and enriched program for pre-service as well as in-service teachers. This involved establishment of an undergraduate and a graduate division. These changes were requested in order to bring the institution into line with the prevailing concept of the role and function of the professional school of education. The new dean of the School of Education had had a significant part in the development of these newer concepts through his pioneering work in the Harris Teachers College, in St. Louis, Missouri, and as superintendent of schools of that city.

The faculty for the School of Education was drawn largely from personnel with both pedagogical training and practical school experience. To insure retention of the liberal arts in the undergraduate program, as well as to insure efficiency in the training of subject-matter teachers, authorization was secured for the incorporation of subject-matter departments into the School of Education. These included English, mathematics, science, and the social studies. Increasing demands for trained personnel within the school system and in the wider community stimulated the professional school to gradually extend its sphere of influence by continually broadening its offerings, ultimately building curricula for nonteaching as well as teaching positions.

The salutary effects of these changes is reflected in the growth of faculty, departments and programs of instruction, and enrollment throughout the years 1921–38, including the period of the great Depression. The degree of success achieved by the revitalized School of Education may be measured in three ways:

1] the vision and leadership demonstrated by the administration,

2] the cooperation and dedication of the faculty, and

3] the demonstrated courage to pioneeer as well as to respond to the ever-changing demands of the culture.

Perhaps the true measure of success of these first fifty years is to be found in the influence the School already was wielding on American education through the placement of its graduates in key positions in education and in wider community responsibilities both throughout this country and in foreign lands. This assumption is supported by Withers in a memorandum to the chancellor in which he notes that between 1921 and 1938 the School of Education awarded 12,811 degrees. In this note he continued:

These graduates are now serving education throughout all parts of the United States and in a number of foreign countries, but the majority of them, especially of those who hold

our doctors' and masters' degrees, are in prominent positions
in education in New York City and the metropolitan area.
. . . These and all other students, those now with us and
those who have been with us within the past seventeen and
a half years, together with all members of the faculty, present
and past, wherever they are and whatever they are doing,
constitute the real School of Education.

CONCLUSIONS

Response to the demands of an ever changing culture,
with instances of pioneering prior to the national impact
of such social pressures, characterizes the emergence and
development of teacher education at New York University
between 1888 and 1938.

The accomplishments of the institution were achieved
during years of stress and challenge. In the twenty years
between the first and second world wars, great ferment
and change occurred in all areas of the University program. In the professional schools deep dissatisfaction pre-
vailed with the curriculum, with the proliferation of
courses, with superficiality, and lack of purpose in the
program as a whole, and throughout this period widespread efforts at reform were undertaken. While the
School of Education was beset by some of these ills,
leadership in American education was demonstrated by
the administration and faculty in seeking reform through
a clear delineation of aims and purposes and through
building a program to implement these goals.

The somewhat detailed report of the first fifty years of
teacher education at New York University has been provided to indicate the process of development in organization, program, and student body. It serves to suggest the
stability which the teacher-training unit achieved within

its first half century. This stability, far from engendering stagnation, has been the foundation upon which to build a stronger and increasingly influential institution devoted to serving those preparing for work in varied professional fields and in an environment no longer confined to the metropolitan area of New York City but reaching into all parts of the world.

In the sections which follow, therefore, less attention will be given to the explicit data which seemed essential to give the reader an insight into the emergence of the institution, and greater emphasis will be placed on those larger issues, both internal and external, which contributed toward shaping its present image.

Part III

The Next Quarter of a Century

7 · The Frenetic Forties— The Fault-Finding Fifties

CONTINUED AGITATION IN THE SOCIAL SCENE

Following one year as acting dean in 1939, Enoch George Payne, who had served Withers first as assistant dean, then as associate dean as well as chairman of the Department of Educational Sociology, succeeded to the deanship of the School of Education. He and the faculty had worked toward and therefore inherited a basically sound administrative and academic foundation. Some foundations outside halls of learning appeared less sound in this fifth decade of the twentieth century. Payne's tenure, though comparatively short (1939–45), was not uneventful.

As in each previous decade, the 1940s witnessed a serious upheaval in the social order. By this time the extreme elements of national socialism seemed to threaten the very roots of civilization and these ominous signs presaged World War II. It was a time also when, as reported by Chancellor Chase, accusations of racial discrimination were beginning to be heard on all sides.[1]

[1] *Annual Report* of the Chancellor to the Council of the University for 1945–46, p. 29.

In the educational milieu statistics indicate that following Pearl Harbor, for various reasons, 100,000, or nearly one tenth of all the teachers in the country, left the profession, and the number of new persons entering the teaching profession annually declined almost as much. It was during this era that curricula of secondary schools and colleges felt the influences of a new stress on science and mathematics, propelled sharply into the limelight by the appearance of the atomic bomb and the first faint rumblings of the space age. In a few years Sputnik gave the real eye-opener to the status of the sciences, and then big things began to happen. In the meantime, revised subject-matter content and a consequent necessity of retraining existing teaching personnel as well as of attracting greater numbers of teachers to these fields created problems for teacher-education institutions. An outgrowth of this situation was a shortage of teachers in science and mathematics and in certain phases of vocational education at the secondary and college levels.

The combination of these pressures, aggravated by such additional problems as gas rationing, paper shortages, restrictions on publications, and so forth, made the years between 1940 and 1946 difficult ones for educational institutions and for the advancement of education. The School of Education, too, had to come to grips with these dilemmas.

THE PAYNE ADMINISTRATION—1939-45

Undeterred by financial and other worries brought about by the war, Dean Payne, his right bower Associate Dean Pickett, and the energetic corps of men and women comprising the faculty went about the serious business of making contributions to the war effort while maintaining the standards of service to the student body and to the profession which had come to characterize this division of the University.

The Program and the Student Body

Obviously the entry of thousands of young men and women into military and other war services was reflected in a reduced enrollment. When Dr. Payne entered upon his new duties in 1939, the enrollment was 12,083. Within four years it had dropped to 6496. Prophetically the dean predicted that this situation would soon reverse itself and that in less than a decade all schools would be taxed to capacity. Even by 1946 the figure for the School of Education had climbed back to 9235, and by the end of the decade it was 13,715, the highest enrollment figure to date.

Throughout the emergency the work of the School was geared toward the war effort. One of the first efforts in this direction was a conference held in April, 1942, under the joint auspices of the School of Education and the United States Commission on Educational Reconstruction. Two significant recommendations came out of this meeting: (1) that an office of cabinet level be set up to foster international education and (2) that an appropriate educational experience be developed for persons between the ages of 18 and 25. At the School of Education there was an attempt to implement this latter point by incorporating in the course offerings a program in adult education. On the home front, the Department of Home

Economics gave special attention to the problems of food rationing, preservation of foods, and nutrition. In the program of the Department of Physical Education, the importance of physical fitness and of recreation was emphasized. A training program for war industries was set up in the Department of Vocational Education under the direction of Professor William P. Sears, Jr., chairman of the department at the time. This was subsidized by state and federal funds and in the first year over more than 1200 persons had completed this special training. By the time the program was terminated, at least 3000 individuals were prepared to contribute to the war efforts in various war industries. In addition, the government reported that the civilian pilot training program, conducted by Professor Roland H. Spaulding under the auspices of the same department, turned out more trained individuals than any other similar program conducted by any other university in the country.

Looking ahead, the School organized courses in occupational therapy and vocational rehabilitation for which there would be increasing demand as the war progressed and after. In the same period, numerous short courses as well as regular courses were designed to upgrade teachers in specific lines and to reeducate others in areas where the demand for updating subject matter was greatest. Not only did such services represent a service to the country, they gave employment to faculty and staff during a difficult period.

From the time he joined the staff, E. George Payne had fostered recognition of racial contributions to cultural development and urged intercultural education. It is not surprising, therefore, especially in the light of growing discontent, to learn that during his tenure two significant steps were taken in this direction. First, under a grant from the General Education Board, there was established a three-year visiting professorship in Negro education and culture. Second, in 1945 negotiations were initiated with the Bureau of Intercultural Education in New York City, which eventuated, with financial assistance from private donors as well as from the Julius Rosenwald Fund, the establishment of the Center for Human Relations in 1947. Dr. H. H. Giles, who had been with the Bureau of Inter-Cultural Education, was the first director. This step made possible intensive graduate research, training, and field work in the educational treatment of conflicts which show themselves in the relationships between religious, racial, social, and economic groups. Over the years the work of this unit has included sociological studies and surveys of communities in New York City and beyond. Several of these projects have been undertaken at the request of municipal agencies seeking assistance in improving conditions in specific areas. In 1954 work in human relations was made available as a formal program of study.

When the impact of the war had eased, a series of seminars were instituted combining the principle of classroom teaching with practical work experience. This, in effect, was the birth of the "workshop" technique. In 1947–48, workshops were conducted in eleven auxiliary centers in addition to those carried on at Washington Square. This comprehensive program included workshops in educational leadership and secondary education, neither of which had ever been given before; another for teachers and supervisors of mentally retarded children conducted in cooperation with the New York City schools; one in human relations carried out through the Center for Human Relations; two in child development; one in contemporary culture for college teachers; and another in community action, the latter in connection with the New York State Citizens' Council.

At Sarah Lawrence College a special curriculum workshop was carried on in problems of economic education for supervisors and administrators in state school systems. This was the first workshop of its kind, and Professor G. Derwood Baker directed it. Dr. Baker was given a prolonged leave of absence to undertake leadership in the development of the Joint Council on Economic Education. In subsequent years workshops in economic education gained popularity in several centers, including Puerto Rico, under the expert direction of Professor S. P. McCutchen. Professor McCutchen also is a member of the Joint Council on Economic Education. A variety of contemporary problems was handled in a similar manner at Chautauqua Institution where for a number of years the University had carried on certain phases of its summer program in teacher training. The range of subject matter covered by the workshops and the increase in the use of this educational technique led Chancellor Chase to note the growing emphasis upon active student participation in problems directly concerned with the realities of the area of study. He characterized the workshop as an extension of the laboratory technique formerly restricted to the physical sciences.

In the same report, the chancellor commented upon an

issue which has come up for consideration in every succeeding decade, including the present one, as later references to the topic will reveal. This was the matter of the liberal arts. Chase stated:

Notwithstanding the spectacular advances of higher education in America in professional and vocational fields of training, the basic liberal arts discipline continues to mark the center of gravity on every university campus. New York University while peculiarly pledged from its inception to practical instruction, has never forsaken faith in the . . . traditional liberal arts studies . . . as foundational preparation for any professional or allied career. Therefore, while these reports stress what we have done in adjusting our diversified curricula to the changing needs of the times, we have not lost sight of our responsibility to cherish and nourish the age-old academic pursuits from which the remarkable foliation of other university activity has stemmed.

With a view to strengthening the undergraduate curriculum and enriching the liberal-cultural portion of it, a subcommittee of the Curriculum Committee was appointed in 1944 to formulate a new core curriculum more appropriate to the contemporary needs of the School of Education. The subcommittee consisted of Professor McCutchen, chairman, and Professors Gabler and Sears. In submitting a suggested core the subcommittee presented the following considerations:

1] The responsibilities that must be shouldered by our students as citizens in a dynamic and changing democracy. Provision has, therefore, been made for the cultural education necessary for all college people to have so that they may aspire to intellectual maturity and to wisdom.

2] Account was also taken of the need for a broad professional background so that our students, as professional people, may acquit themselves with honor and dignity, with competence and efficiency.

3] Account was also taken for the need of specialized and technical training so that our students might be prepared thoroughly for effective participation in the work of the world.

The proposed core plan grouped studies under four headings:

Group   I. Education for the Common Life
Group   II. Education for Professional Life
Group III. Education for the Field of Specialization
Group   IV. Electives

The special subcommittee recommended that the proposed core, if adopted, be approved for no more than three years and that during that time study and evaluation of the core be continued. The subcommittee's proposals and recommendations were accepted by the faculty in 1945.

An educational imperative which emerged during the decade of the second world war was the need of providing learning opportunities for the adult population. The reconstruction of our democratic life, in the wake of changes brought on partly by the war and partly by scientific developments of the twentieth century, compelled such opportunities for adults controlled by nineteenth century habits of thought and action in a twentieth century world. Adult education as a formal part of the School's offerings received careful scrutiny and planning within this and the following decade under the direction of a staunch exponent, Dr. John Carr Duff.

Fresh from his experiences with the *Eight-Year Study* which had evaluated the relationships between secondary school and college programs, Dr. McCutchen took over the chairmanship of the Department of the Social Studies in 1943. Under his leadership the department grew in size, quality, and curricular innovations both in theory and practice. For example, Dr. McCutchen has devoted much of his professional endeavors to perfecting a technique for meaningful teaching of the social studies commonly referred to as the "problems approach." Through his writings, including several texts, and his numerous consultantships as well as through the application of this technique by his former students, the "problems approach" has gained considerable acceptance and adoption. Professor McCutchen, throughout his University association, has given statesman-like leadership to the institution, not only as chairman of the Social Studies Department, but in such roles as chairman of the Graduate Committee and chairman of committees and subcommittees concerned with raising undergraduate and graduate work to new levels of quality. Currently, Dr. McCutchen is chairman of the elected members of the University senate.

The Department of Early Childhood and Elementary Education added in 1949 its graduate pre-service program (125A) for students who had majored in some field other than elementary or early childhood education in their undergraduate studies. The course was planned to develop the personal and professional attributes essential to elementary school teachers for the important responsibility of influencing the lives of children.

Internal Activities During the 1940s

The added responsibilities imposed by the war years

did not lessen the interests of the faculty in institutional affairs. Faculty committees produced, before the decade was half over, three proposals intended to improve the structure and services of the teacher-education division. These proposals related to (1) faculty reorganization clarifying the distinctions between administrative and legislative functions, (2) the policies looking toward the gradual development of a functional program of guidance, and (3) recommendations for the revision of the under-graduate program with special reference to the core curriculum which was coming into wider acceptance in this country. Reference to this latter item already has been made. As to number one, there were two developments: The faculty organization which was proposed in 1945, while retaining the overall committee structure adopted in 1926, called for changes in title and function of certain existing committees and for the addition of others. Thus, for example, the former General Committee was to be designated as Committee on General Policy and was to include in its areas of responsibility faculty welfare and promotions. Inclusion of this area would have made it unnecessary to continue the existing Committee of Seven.

In voting upon the proposal, the faculty deleted this area from the functions of the Committee on General Policy. Committees on graduate study, undergraduate study, and alumni and public relations were continued.

A Committee on Business Management was added with responsibility for:

      1] budget,
      2] office space and office services,
      3] building service, and
      4] registration procedures.

The method of election to the Committee on General Policy was by secret proportional representation. A Committee on Committees was added to nominate the committee personnel for each of the standing committees.

A second structural change grew out of the fact that several units of the university sustained a loss of teaching personnel between 1942 and 1945. This led to issuance by the University administration of a directive increasing the teaching load from twelve to fifteen hours for all full-time faculty members. It was the consensus of the School of Education personnel that this action pointed up a gap in communication between faculty and administration about which something should be done. It did not take too long before something was done. Spearheaded by several of the more articulate members of the faculty, offices, conference rooms, and hallways echoed lively, sometimes heated, discussions of the means by which policy was arrived at in the University, especially as such policies affected faculty—administration relationships. This group included Dr. Samuel L. Hamilton, chairman of the Department of Religious Education; Dr. Alonzo F. Myers, of the Department of Higher Education; and Dr. Robert K. Speer, chairman of the Department of Elementary Education—a triumvirate difficult to beat when matters of faculty welfare were at stake. Out of these deliberations emerged the Committee of Seven to cooperate with the administration and to bring, either to the appropriate standing committees or directly to the faculty for consideration, any problem legally belonging to the faculty. The formulation of this committee was the first breakthrough in (1) provision for recourse in the event of a grievance on the part of a faculty member and (2) more direct involvement of the faculty in matters of policy. Professor Ernest R. Wood, a member of the Department of Educational Psychology, was elected chairman. His mild, almost shy manner belied his statesmanship.

The committee's first order of business was to study its potential functions in relation to the statutes of New York University and the existing organization of the School of Education. A letter from the committee to the faculty, dated February 2, 1944, sought answers to three questions: (1) what general functions the committee should perform for the School, (2) what long-range objectives the institution should seek to achieve during the war years and in the transition period which would follow, and (3) what were the immediate problems in relation to these long-range objectives.

Serving in a liaison capacity, the committee sought authorization to communicate directly with the faculty, but on February 4, 1944, the dean wrote:

> . . . I note also the request that the statement be sent. I have received your proposed communication to the faculty from your committee and I think it is excellently formed and ought to bring out important information.
>
> I note also the request that the statement be sent without my approval. This is a request impossible to grant. All communications going to the faculty over this desk must be with my approval since I am held responsible by the administration for all communications. . . .

Based on the knowledge that Payne's retirement was imminent, one of the first acts of the Committee of Seven was to file with the chancellor, at his request, the following statement of desirable qualifications and characteristics to be sought in the next dean:

1] He should possess recognized standing, scholarship and experience in professional teacher-education.

2] His personality and his ability to speak and write should permit him to represent the School of Education favorably to other divisions within the University, to other academic groups, and to the general public.

3] His age, physical stamina, and mental alertness should give promise that he will be able to lead the School of Education aggressively for at least fifteen to twenty years without mental or physical flagging.

4] He should be a maturely balanced individual who is at the same time warmly human in his professional relationships and objective in his judgments of persons and issues.

5] He should be able to take opposition in matters of principle without assuming that such opposition constitutes disloyalty.

6] He should have demonstrated skill in the use of cooperative procedures in reaching administrative decisions.

7] He should have demonstrated ability to work as an administrator within the complex structure of a University.

8] He should be able to develop excellent morale in the members of the faculty, students and alumni.

9] He should be able to recognize and encourage superior ability in the members of his staff, especially superior ability in teaching and in research.

10] He should have given evidence of social vision through participation in significant movements of public welfare.

11] He should have demonstrated interest in the complex social problems of American democracy and be unmistakably free from prejudice toward any particular class, race, or religion.

12] He should have knowledge of and experience in dealing with the special problems of a larger urban community.

13] He should have shown awareness of the relationship between the educational problems of America and of the rest of the world.

The chancellor's acknowledgement of this communication was addressed to the chairman and read:

I want to thank you and your committee for the fine work which has been done in drawing up the list of qualifications desirable in a new dean for the School of Education. I regard it as the best balanced list of qualifications for an administrative position that has come my way in a long time. It will be very helpful to me in moving on with the matter.[2]

Between February, 1944 and April, 1945, this commitee held twenty-six regular meetings, two special meetings with the chancellor, and also arranged three meetings between the faculty and candidates for the deanship. In time the name of this group was changed to the Committee on Faculty Welfare and Administrative Relations. Over the past twenty years its role has broadened to include consideration of such matters as salaries, fringe benefits, curricular and instructional innovations, and the continued extension of faculty participation in policy making, not only at the local school, but at the University level.

Forrest E. Long, of the Department of Secondary Education, was among the highly motivated and active group of faculty members who were sensitive to the need for achieving greater security and professional status for all faculty members. As the elected School of Education representative on the University senate, Long worked assiduously to achieve significant revisions in appointment and tenure regulations. He was able to see the fruits of these efforts within the decade.

Keen interest in the development of a more functional program of guidance at both the undergraduate and graduate levels led to several reviews throughout the forties and fifties of this area of activity. Basic policies for the

[2] *Letter* from H. W. Chase, Chancellor, to E. R. Wood, chairman, Committee of Seven, dated November 16, 1944.

student personnel program were set forth in a report entitled *Principles and Objectives of the Guidance Program,* prepared by a committee under the chairmanship of Dr. McCutchen. This report was approved by the faculty in the spring of 1945.

It is of interest to note that the oldest existing policy is the policy on student government as set forth in the "Charter for Student Activities" adopted by the faculty in 1930.

Refinements and additions of the *Principles and Objectives of Guidance* were made by faculty committees from time to time. Such additions included "Policy and Program for Student Health," 1948, Dr. Forrest E. Long, chairman. In 1955 this school policy was superseded by a University Health Service. In 1951 a "Scholarship Policy and Program" was approved; the committee which prepared this proposal was chaired by Dr. George Axtelle, chairman of the Department of Philosophy of Education. A system of general orientation and advisement for sixth-year and doctoral applicants was instituted in 1955 with Dean Florence Beaman, chairman. Student probation and discipline policies were revised in 1956, also under Dean Beaman. Since 1948 the faculty committees concerned with student affairs have looked to Dean Beaman, assistant dean in charge of students, for stimulating and perceptive guidance and leadership.

The "Charter for Student Activities" represented a unique and forward movement in student participation, especially when one notes the year of its adoption, 1930.

In the closing paragraphs of his annual report for 1942–43, Dean Payne noted that at the end of the succeeding year he would have served the University twenty-two years. He offered two reasons for seeking retirement: He wrote:

First, I came to New York University when the School of Education was first organized and have participated in every act of its development in becoming one of the leading schools of its kind.

Second, since this is the beginning of a new era of development in the School of Education and since the leadership must be placed in someone else's hands, my successor ought to have the opportunity to be responsible from the beginning to plan and create the program for the new era.

Since my personality and life has gone into this School it will continue to be my dominant interest, and without intrusion I shall aid it indirectly in the future to fulfill its potential role.

The faculty of the School of Education and the central University administration deliberated on the matter of a successor for almost two years. Dean Payne continued to serve the institution through August 31, 1945.

Following his retirement, Dean Payne continued to assist needy students to secure a college education, an endeavor he had privately carried on for many years. In addition he devoted much time and energy to the Save the Children Foundation, an agency engaged in salvaging the lives of children made parentless and/or homeless by the second world war and subsequent military events in the Far East.

Dr. Ernest O. Melby, then president of Montana State University at Missoula, was invited to accept the position at New York University. He assumed the deanship of the School of Education on September 1, 1945.

DEAN MELBY'S TENURE—1945–56

Postwar Conditions

The term "postwar" is hardly an accurate description of the period since 1945. Shortly after World War II was officially ended, the thirty-eighth parallel running through Korea became a symbol for civil wars which, starting in Korea, have continued to erupt on several continents of a world in revolt.

Two years after VJ-Day a hurried glance back would have revealed that the first two years of peace were far from peaceful. In fact, the international signs and domestic developments were so disturbing that defeatism might well have engulfed the human spirit.

Instead, Americans faced the sobering realization that this nation would be called upon to take worldwide leadership in the preservation of peace and the furtherance of human values. The obligation was not one to be taken lightly and the magnitude of it could not help but turn the search light of inquiry on education.

Since mid-twentieth century, the status of American education has been the subject of considerable discussion in the professional and lay press. Numerous books, articles, pamphlets, radio programs, and television panels have bombarded the public with accounts of the pedagogical ills besetting the nation's schools and colleges. Acceleration in such discussion appeared in the years immediately following the second World War and contained the makings of the deepest educational crisis in the nation's history. This critical assault put education on the defensive and, in the opinion of certain educators, made it imperative that the strength and weaknesses of our educational tradition be reassessed.

While Dean Melby responded through the professional press to some of the charges leveled against teacher education, neither he nor the faculty ignored the fact that a society changing as rapidly as theirs demanded constant adaptation and modification of instruction if the institution preparing the teacher was going to turn out teachers fitted to meet the challenges of the times.

Program Revisions and Innovations

In this spirit, then, there was once again critical examination of the work of the School of Education at both the undergraduate and the graduate levels.

Professors Iglehart, Kinsella, Mayfarth, Raths, Zorbaugh, and Rockwell as chairman, worked as a special committee from 1950 to 1953 in a search for a structural design in which the curricula of the school would be knit together in more meaningful ways. Dean Melby further suggested that it was his hope that such a design would make it possible to utilize better the talents of the faculty.

The committee expressed the belief that a school such as this, located in the largest city in the world, with the varied competencies represented on its staff and at its doorstep, should be able to accomplish educational objectives which other institutions would find it difficult to attain.

An outgrowth of this study was "the five-year look" which envisaged the master's degree as a fifth year of preparation for teaching. The recommendations of this report popularly referred to as the "blue book" were, for the most part, implemented in 1953. Despite the new wave of charges of anti-intellectualism and over-professionalization which appeared in the early 1950s, the idea of an integrated program of general basic education was not new to American education or to the School of Education of New York University. Concern with possible overemphasis on the vocational development of the student at the expense of the cultural was evident in the 1940s. The School of Education, as previously noted, made its first attempt to avoid such a charge in 1928 when it secured approval to include liberal arts subjects within its own program. The offerings in general education in the School of Education were reviewed in 1940, 1947, and 1953. The question of the place and function of the liberal arts in the undergraduate curriculum persisted, however, into the next decade when the University as a whole participated in the development of a program of coordinated liberal studies.

The turn of the decade ushered in the GI Bill of Rights and, with it, certain changes which may have permanently influenced American education. This bill was a fitting gesture on the part of a grateful nation. It did several things. It permitted those whose education might have been interrupted by military service to complete work for a baccalaureate or an advanced degree. It enabled those who couldn't otherwise afford to go to college to do so. To some extent it required colleges and universities to accommodate their procedures to the terms of the bill. For better or worse, it reinforced the idea that practically every individual born in this country should go to college and, by further implication, that this opportunity should be made available through some form of financial support where need could be demonstrated.

So far as the School of Education was concerned, the enrollment picture between 1940 and 1959 is an erratic one. For example, just prior to World War II the enrollment was 11,632. By 1944 it had dropped to 6496. In 1946 there were 9235 students enrolled and for the next several years the import of the GI bill is clear in the following figures:

Year	Enrollment
1954	8490
1953	9809
1952	11,709
1951	13,029
1950	13,715
1949	12,826
1948	12,219
1947	11,040

Through the drop-out of students who were unsuccessful, lost interest, married, became restless, or whose funds ran out, college enrollment leveled off following the peak years of the GI bill. For the School of Education this has remained between 6000 and 7000 registrants annually.

Organizational Changes

The administration of the School of Education during the Melby regime consisted of the dean assisted by Associate Dean Pickett, Associate Dean Rosecrance who joined the staff in 1946, and Assistant Dean Beaman. Dr. Peter L. Agnew functioned as assistant dean with responsibility for budget and personnel matters from 1948 through 1954. Five significant changes were introduced in the School of Education during Dean Melby's tenure. The first of these was dictated by the fact that outside calls for assistance and leadership were assuming such proportions that the need for centralizing these responsibilities became apparent. This was accomplished by establishing the Center for Community Studies and Field Services. The center began formal operation in 1947.

In the early years of the center, requests for professional help came primarily from New York City agencies and neighborhoods. These services soon extended to communities in the metropolitan area and adjacent states. Today this unit is called the Center for School Services and Off-Campus Courses. The total cost of service contracts negotiated through the center in 1963–64 was approximately $250,000—a ten-fold increase over the previous year. The number of professors who participated in activities of the center during the same year increased markedly to 102. Through various departments 65 courses were offered in 27 centers.

The second event of significance was the inauguration of the Puerto Rican program. Although Professor Robert K. Speer broke ground for bringing New York University to Puerto Rico by conducting two workshops on the island in 1948 and 1949, a genuine experiment in cross-cultural education was launched when the first comprehensive Puerto Rican program was offered at Rio Piedras, Puerto Rico in 1952.

From the small number of courses offered in 1948, restricted primarily to the work of Dr. Pauline Rojas in

English as a second language, the intersession program at Puerto Rico has steadily grown.

In April, 1961 a resident center for the School of Education's graduate program in Puerto Rico was established at the University of Puerto Rico in Rio Piedras. Since 1952 the Directors of the Puerto Rican Program have been:

Walter A. Anderson	1952–58 inclusive
Samuel P. McCutchen	1959–60
John C. Payne (Parmer L. Ewing, acting in Payne's absence)	1961–62
Parmer L. Ewing	1963
Robert W. Clausen	1964

In June 1964, 340 studnts were enrolled. To date some 60 faculty members have taken part in the Puerto Rican program. About 600 master's degrees have been awarded and eight candidates have earned doctor's degrees. Later reference to faculty participation will reveal additional services rendered to the commonwealth by members of the faculty of the School of Education.

By 1951, recognizing the growth in numbers, complexity, and importance of doctoral work in the School of Education, the faculty had proposed establishment of a Division for the Scientific Study and Advancement of Education, with a full-time director, but not *separate* full-time faculty. This division, constituting a third change in organization, began operation as of September, 1952 with Dr. Alonzo G. Grace, appointed to serve as associate dean and director of the division.

Perhaps an apt phrase to sum up Melby's philosophy is one he himself frequently used, namely, "mobilizing the total resources."

These words, he believed, represented the function and responsibility of education. He viewed them as applying with equal significance to the operation of the School of Education as to the whole field of education. Consequently, shortly after taking up his duties, he directed his attention to the problem of unifying and coordinating the program and activities of the institution.

In his annual report for 1946–47 he wrote to the chancellor:

If the problems in the field are to be met, we must bring to bear all of the various talents we possess and our resources must be marshalled without regard to the departmental location of individual staff members.

Internally the organization is equally confusing. Neither the problems of school systems nor of individual students can be solved by 28 independent departments often making conflicting demands upon the student.

As a result of the dean's conviction that a complete reorganization of the School was essential, a totally new pattern of organization emerged. On May 14, 1952 the dean issued a memorandum addressed to the members of the faculty in which he said:

After giving thoughtful consideration to all suggestions received, I have prepared the attached statement of the administrative organization under which we will operate beginning September 1, 1952. Insofar as planning for the school year 1953–54 and thereafter is concerned, the plan goes into effect immediately.

The scheme grouped departments and functions under three titular divisions each under the supervision of an assiociate dean, as follows:

1] Division of General Teacher Education, Community and Field Services—Associate Dean Rosecrance;

2] Division of Professional Studies in the Fine and Practical Arts and other Special Areas—Associate Dean Pickett; and

3] Division of the Scientific Study and Advancement of Education—Associate Dean Grace.

The paucity of faculty participation in this plan, its adoption through administrative directive, and possibly operation of the adage "there's nothing so changeless as change," saw this structure abandoned within four years when once again the chain of command passed into new hands.

Finally, in 1951 there was added a Sixth-Year Post-Master's Program leading to a certificate as Specialist in Education. This enabled persons, not interested in earning a doctorate, but desirous of doing advanced graduate work or of qualifying for increment by completing 30 points of work beyond a master's degree, to follow a planned program instead of simply amassing 30 points with no educational rationale or professional objective. Here again, the program called for a proportion of the courses to be in liberal-cultural subjects.

In its first seventeen years as the School of Education, the teacher-education division of New York University presented a phenomenal record of growth and of vision in opening up new vistas in professional education.

This spirit of pioneering and progress was amply sustained in its next seventeen. The labors of the administrative officers and faculty between 1939 and 1956 bore such fruits as:

1] establishment of the Committee of Seven, now the Committee on Faculty Welfare and Administrative Relations,

2] establishment of the Center for Human Relations,

3] establishment of the Center for Community Studies and Field Services,

4] development of a program of studies in Puerto Rico,

5] Such curricular and structural innovations as adoption of the "blue book" (the five-year look),

6] an experiment in an administrative reorganization of the School from which the Division of Advanced Study has survived, and

7] addition of the Sixth-Year Program.

These were not quiet years—neither externally in the world at large, nor internally within the profession of education—nay, even within the walls of the School of Education.

True to his philosophy to the end, in his last report to the president, Melby voiced the sentiment that the greatest weakness on the educational front was not a lack of teachers or buildings, serious as these might be, but lack of a plan and process for mobilizing the resources of education. He cited three major obstacles to achieving this goal: public lack of understanding and resultant apathy, administrative inadequacy, and shortage of properly prepared personnel.

Perhaps, growing out of certain experiences during his eleven year tenure, he deplored the fact that in the 1920s, ". . . we developed a concept of administration which seems to make it professional malpractice for an administrator to make a decision. What sets out to be democratic

administration becomes a slow-moving oppressive collec-
tivism which functions largely as a defense of the status
quo." [3] This view did not find universal agreement among
the members of the faculty. But neither opposing philosophies, nor the trials and errors which went into the
attempts to resolve them, impeded the efforts of the institution toward continued enlargement of its sphere of
influence.

The incessant dictates of time, however, once again
required selection of a successor as administrative head.

In this decade of stern chastisement of education, New
York University in 1953 decided to conduct a three-year,
major self-study. Dr. George D. Stoddard, whose distinguished record in education had been capped by the
presidency of the University of Illinois, was the man
chosen to guide and direct this important undertaking.
The final report of the self-study was in process of completion when Dr. Stoddard was invited to fill the vacancy
in the School of Education. On September 1, 1956, sixty-
six years after it was founded, Dr. Stoddard became the
institution's seventh dean.

THE TRANSITION YEARS WITH DEAN STODDARD—1956–59

The recommendations of the recently completed self-
study were used by the new administrative head of the
teacher-education unit as a basis for what he termed the
School of Education in transition.

Assisting Dean Stoddard in the increasingly complex
responsibilities of administering the School were Associate

[3] *Annual Report*, of the dean to the President for 1955–56, p. 11.

Dean Pickett, working on space allocation, Lake Sebago (the site of the University physical education camp), travel plans, and serving as director of the summer session; Associate Dean Grace, in charge of all research and advanced programs on or off the campus and director of the Division of Advanced Study; and Assistant Dean Beaman, in charge of students. Following the resignation of Associate Dean Rosecrance in 1956, Professor Walter A. Anderson, formerly chairman of the Department of Administration and Supervision, joined the administrative staff as associate dean. He served as acting dean during the dean's absence, and matters of staff and budget were in his hands.

One of the self-study recommendations called for establishment of an Experimental Teaching Center as a part of the School of Education. Such a center, with Professor Glen Heathers of the Department of Educational Psychology as director, began formal operation in 1958. Its first major project was called the dual progress plan. Two school systems on Long Island participated in the experiment. Under the dual progress plan pupils in grades one through six remain with a homeroom teacher for half a day. This time is devoted to reading, writing, speech, and the social studies. The remainder of the day is spent under special teachers of mathematics, science, music, arts and crafts, recreation, and health. Under the plan a pupil's grade standing (an overall maturity concept) is determined by his homeroom teacher, but the pupil is free to pursue a specialty according to his aptitude and rate of achievement. The Experimental Teaching Center affords a unique opportunity for graduate students, teachers, professors, and administrators to evaluate proposed changes in theory and practice.

In his second annual report Dean Stoddard stated:

Last year we emphasized quality and variety as key concepts in the School's program. Now that everything under the banner of Education is under fire from one quarter or another, we should like to add a third—*originality*. In all three qualities it is pleasant to record that the entire faculty is moving forward as a team.

A significant forward step was taken in 1957–58 with ten teaching fellowships made available for advanced study. The fellowships carried an allowance of $2500 each, together with tuition remission. With this assistance, a graduate student could take a leave of absence from his position to work on an advanced degree in the School of Education.

Between 1956 and 1959 such additional changes took place as:

1] a reduction in the total number of departments in the School through consolidations,

2] introduction of the Integrated Program in Teacher Education for Liberal Arts Graduates (Graduate Program 891),

3] installation of a graduate program in the field of the Creative Arts (610 C) designed to enable students to further their understanding of the nature of creativity and to enrich the conceptual bases of their expression through course work in the liberal arts and especially in aesthetics,

4] acceptance of the "blue book" plan of curricula by the New York State Department of Education, and

5] inauguration of a sixth-year program in the Department of Administration and Supervision, conducted by the School of Education at Hofstra College, Hempstead, Long Island.

6] In November, 1957 the School of Education joined with 33 other major institutions in establishing the University Council for Educational Administration. The council was concerned with research and preparation programs in educational administration. The United States Office of Education approved a grant of $261,000 to the council. The project was scheduled to run three years and was to deal with criteria for selecting school administrators and evaluating their work. Recognition of the high competencies within the School of Education faculty was evidenced in the appointment of Associate Dean Anderson as a member of the Executive Committee of the newly formed council. He was elected to the presidency of the organization in the next year.

Towards the end of the 1950s the offerings overseas grew in geographic areas covered as well as number of students enrolled. As of this writing four such programs have been offered for ten or more consecutive summers:

Director C.O. Arndt,	The Seminar on Western Europe	(First year 1950)
Director A.I. Katsh,	The Land of the Bible (Israel)	(First year 1952)
Directors Anderson, McCutchen, Payne, Ewing, Clausen	The Intercession Program in Puerto Rico	(First year 1948)
Directors Speer, Giles, Dossick, Carras	Workshop for school people from the Mainland to Puerto Rico	(First year 1947)

Faculty commissions abroad increased markedly, and in 1959 Professor William Brickman, a member of the Department of Philosophy and History of Education, attended the International Conference on Educational Research in Tokyo. This conference was sponsored by the Japan Society for The Study of Education. Dean Stoddard spent ten weeks in Korea reporting for the International Cooperation Administration on United States commitments in Korean higher education, with particular reference to Seoul National University. Professor W. C. Spencer of the Department of Higher Education served in Chile as consultant to the United Nations, and Professor A. J. Foy Cross, of the Department of Secondary Education, was in Peru with the United States Educational Commission.

An Advisory Council for the School of Education was approved in the Fall of 1959. The preamble to the proposal stated:

The School of Education of New York University is a major educational center. Over 6000 students and about 200 full-time faculty members are involved. The impact that the School of Education—faculty members, alumni, and students —has had on state, national, and world educational problems is well known.

The complex problems facing education at all levels create a major challenge to the School of Education. Because of the significant record of the School in the past, many feel an even greater potential contribution could be made in the future. In order to render the most effective leadership in educational circles, the School needs the best advice and counsel it is possible to obtain. Hence, it is proposed that a council be created to serve in an advisory capacity to the faculty and administration.

The report continues:

The purpose of the Advisory Council for the School of Education is to serve as a sympathetic group that will give advice and aid so that the School of Education can better achieve its educational objectives.

The Advisory Council will act as a sounding board for ideas and plans; discuss ways and means for the School of Education to obtain needed facilities, faculty, and scholarships; and aid in public relations.

This agency still functions. Committee membership is drawn from such sources as alumni, professional education, business, and public service. In addition to nine members from these sources, the dean, chairman of the faculty council, and the School of Education representative to the University senate serve in an *ex officio* capacity, without vote.

RESUMÉ

Crowded, hectic, active, frustrating, and rewarding are all adjectives which could be used to describe the twenty years between 1940 and 1960. The terms could be applied to the institutional as well as the cultural affairs of the epoch.

The School of Education underwent some radical changes in the span of a generation, some of them dictated by the economic-social conditions, such as the addition of the Center for Human Relations. Other developments resulted from a changing philosophy of education such as the adoption of a basically revised core curriculum for the undergraduates. Still others reflected the coming of age of the School of Education as indicated by the widening demand for expert assistance by School of Education personnel from far-flung corners of the world.

The acceptance of the master's degree as a fifth year in teacher preparation brought with it reappraisal of the service to post master's candidates. The addition of the Sixth-Year Program and a two-year critical review of doctoral policies, leading to major modifications of procedures at this level, are evidences of alertness on the part of the faculty to continue an upgrading of the division. If this array of shifts, changes, additions, and repeated overhaulings of academic affairs leaves the reader breathless—if not confused—it should be borne in mind that evolution is a series of small revolutions.

The Student Life Program, embracing the student activities overall program; the Undergraduate Student Council; and, since 1949, the Graduate Students Organization all brought and continue to bring professional and cultural services and experiences to the student body, including the dual opportunities for self-government and for active participation to a degree that makes the student feel he is, indeed, an integral part of the school of his choice.

The addition of a program in creative arts, permitting the graduate student to incorporate the production of an art form into a professional program in art, is indeed evidence that vision and the will to pioneer still motivate administrators and faculty in this teacher-education organization.

Clearly such achievements were not accomplished through automation. They were accomplished by men and women willing to give unlimited time and energy to the fulfillment of their convictions. Some already have been identified. There also is Alice V. Keliher, who enjoys an established reputation in the field of early childhood education and who worked tirelessly to gain recognition of the area of human relations in the total program of education. Also, believing as she did in the professional value of a tailor-made program of studies for those not wishing to embark on the more rigorous demands of the doctorate, she was a persistent and persuasive member of the committee which finally evolved the Sixth-Year Program.

The important responsibility for the selection of high caliber candidates for the doctorates has been vested in the Committee on Selection and Recommendation of Doctoral Candidates. Throughout the 1940s and 1950s this committee has carried out its functions under the leadership of such men of vision and high purpose as: Dr. Paul V. West, member of the Department of Education Psychology who developed several of the early selection instruments; Professor A. E. Meyer, author and outstanding authority on the history of education; Dr. Leonard A. Larson, who served a term of office as chairman, successor to Dr. Nash as chairman of the Department of Physical Education, Health and Recreation; and Professor Edward L. Kemp, present chairman of the Department of Education Psychology. During the tenures of Doctors Larson and Kemp, major evaluation of the selection process was carried out with the cooperation of the psychological corporation. Professor William P. Sears, Jr. has carried out the responsibilities of the chairmanship of this committee with distinction for the past ten years. The onus for guarding the high quality of doctoral research has rested with the Committee on Doctoral Research Design. Under several designations, this committee has functioned over the years with faculty members from various departments forming the reviewing panels. These groups have worked under the scholarly direction of such chairmen as: Professor A. B. Meredith, chairman of the Graduate Committee from 1930 to 1941; Professor A. D. Whitman, a member of the Department of Secondary Education who served an interim period as chairman of the Graduate Committee; Professor E. L. Kemp, of the Department of Educational Psychology; Professor John C. Payne, then on the staff of the Social Studies Department; Professor Everett Lyne, of the Department of Science Education who gave seven years of uniterrupted service to this task; and the present chairman, Professor James H. Hanscom, who has been active in involving the entire faculty in the problems of research design through faculty seminars and the development of forms to be used in the evaluation of research designs.

Forrest E. Long, of the Department of Secondary Education, was among the highly motivated and active group of faculty members who were sensitive to the need for achieving greater security and professional status for all faculty members. As the elected School of Education representative on the University senate, Long worked assiduously to achieve significant revisions in appointment and tenure regulations. He was able to see the fruits of these efforts within the decade.

Since Dr. Long's term in the University senate, Professors Myers, Payne, and McCutchen have filled this office, with the latter continuing in office for the year 1964–65.

Each man, in turn, has been instrumental in securing improvements in teaching load, pension benefits, life insurance, health insurance, and optional extension of the retirement age. These achievements have constituted University-wide contributions.

Professor G. Derwood Baker, current chairman of the New York University chapter of the American Association of University Professors, and Professor Roscoe Brown, presently chairman of the Committee on Faculty Welfare and Administrative Relations, continue the precedents set by their predecessors in combining their resources within the faculty in order to protect and move forward the professional recognition and reward of those who have made education a life career.

No record of the School of Education would be complete without acknowledging the contribution of Mrs. Ruth T. Shafer who administered the voluminous and complex affairs of the Office of Admissions with outstanding distinction for thirty years. Through her expert direction this office expedited the work of advisers and faculty generally, and through her own personal warmth she did much to enhance the reputation of the School for individual interest and attention.

In the midst of this era of transition Dr. Henry T. Heald, whose title had been changed from chancellor to president of New York University and the Board of Trustees (formerly the Council of the University), drafted Dean Stoddard to serve as chancellor and executive vice-president of the University. This assignment was to begin in September, 1960.

The deanship passed to Dr. Walter A. Anderson, the

present incumbent in that office. This brings us down to the four years preceding the School's Diamond Jubilee. From here on we shall try to examine the record from the point of view of implications for the future of the School of Education as it moves on from its seventy-fifth anniversary to the challenge and excitement of rounding out its first century.

8 · *Here and Now With Anderson—1960—*

The founding fathers would find it difficult to recognize in the complex, multi-purpose School of Education of today their pioneering experiment in teacher training at the university level.

Efficient operation of an organization of this size requires a large staff and the latest technological aids.

Dean Anderson shares the arduous task of administering the division with two associate deans, two assistant deans, and five assistants who carry out particular administrative functions. Associate Dean Payne, a nephew of the former Dean E. George Payne, is in charge of undergraduate instruction. In addition he is director of New York University summer sessions. Upon assumption of this responsibility, he relinquished the directorship of the School of Education summer session to Professor Elmer E. Baker, Jr., chairman of the Department of English and Speech Education.

Assistant Dean Beaman continues to be concerned with the welfare of the student body which requires, among many other things, arrangements for faculty advisement, student counseling and student activities, and registration procedures.

A sure sign of the times is the delegation to Morey R. Fields of the task of fund raising, especially as this relates to the projected new School of Education building and the hoped for New York University School for Children. Professor Fields left the chairmanship of the Department of Physical Education, Health and Recreation to assume the duties of assistant dean in 1962.

Another significant indication of trends in higher education was the appointment, in 1961, of Daniel E. Griffiths as associate dean in charge of doctoral and Sixth-Year Programs and all research programs and projects. Dean Griffiths views the development of a favorable environment for research and the stimulation of research and traineeship proposals as the major focus of his work.

THE CHANGING FACE OF ACADEMIC ACTIVITY

The pressing needs of today's world have made the lot of the educator heavier, more intellectually and physically taxing, but infinitely more dynamic than was the lot of his predecessor. Requests for expert assistance throughout the world, for leadership in national and professional organizations, and the surge in research activity are all parts of the normal expectancy for the college professor and administrator of the 1960s. The horizon of the graduate student also is widening in the light of these cultural developments.

To date at least fifteen members of the staff have worked on one or more occasions with foreign educational agencies in Chile and Peru in South America; Ghana, Nigeria, and Somalia in Africa (the Somalia assignment was part of the Peace Corps program); India, Indonesia, Iran, Israel, Japan, and Korea in the East and Middle East; and Germany, Russia, and Turkey in Europe.

In addition to previously named personnel, faculty members involved in these assignments included: Professors Agnew and Atkinson, from business education; Dean Anderson, representing the administration; Associate Dean Payne, from social studies; Professors G. D. Baker, Robertson and Van Til, working on problems of secondary education; and Professors Chusid (music education), Conant (art education); Belford (religious education), Giles (social studies), and Schwartz (science education) all serving for their respective disciplines. The breadth of faculty competencies represented in this group gives an indication of the range of calls upon the School of Education.

These experiences provide excellent bases for the enrichment of class materials for the students back home and for the promotion of intercultural education. The reputation of the School of Education abroad has been enhanced by the quality of service and leadership which these ambassadors of the School have brought to nations struggling to improve their conditions by improving their educational systems.

Faculty Participation

Looking back in the record there has been no time when the men and women of this division were not active in reading papers before annual conventions and learned societies. In recent years the number of personnel holding top positions in national professional organizations has been growing. Thirty-two members of the faculty will hold such key positions in the coming academic year of 1964-65.

In the area of research, Dean Griffiths reports that forty-four projects were in full operation in 1963-64, and practically all of these are funded for 1964-5. At this writing six additional proposals have been approved for next year and discussions are pending on fifteen others.

Significant activities outside the institution have long commanded the abilities and energies of the staff of this School. As early as 1930, Albert B. Meredith chaired a committee responsible for two volumes of a thirteen-volume report resulting from the White House Conference on Child Health and Protection. In the same decade Meredith held a key position on the New York State Board of Regents Inquiry into the Cost and Character of Higher Education in New York State.

In 1943 an institute was held under the joint auspices of New York University and the United States Committee on Educational Reconstruction, of which committee Professor Reinhold Schairer was executive director. This institute was held at the request of the Central Eastern and European Planning Board of the governments-in-exile of Czechoslavia, Greece, Poland, and Yugoslavia. As a result of this conference the United States Department of State assigned a representative to work unofficially with the committee since it was recognized as the only one with a definite program that had possibilities for specific and effective accomplishments.

In the following decade twenty-five faculty members

participated in Study IV on Economics and Savings in New York State Education for the New York State Education Department.

The Center for Community Services and Off-Campus Courses is a genuine liaison between the educational nucleus and the community. The expansion of this service is obvious from data submitted by Professor Lou Kleinman, the director. He reports contracts negotiated in the past year in the amount of $250,000, a ten-fold increase in the range of participation over the combined five-year period 1957–62.

A comprehensive study of personnel policies for the New York City schools was made at the request of the New York City Board of Education. Expert consultantships were provided for educational surveys in regions within and beyond New York State.

Two major undertakings involving faculty participation were the survey of education in Puerto Rico, which utilized six New York University staff members and sixty-four Puerto Rican educators; and a three-year evaluative study of education in the Virgin Islands currently in progress under the supervision of Professor Edward Dejnozka of the Department of Administration and Supervision. Representatives from practically every department in the School of Education will have spent from one to four months in the Virgin Islands before this study is concluded.

Recent years have seen several curriculum developments geared to the fast-moving age in which we live. The Department of Science and Mathematics Education has girded itself for the space age by redesigning basic science courses and has increased graduate course offerings in content through cooperation with the Science and Mathematics Departments of Washington Square College and the Graduate School of Arts and Science.

A course in *Higher Education* and *World Affairs* was offered through the Department of Higher Education.

Undergraduate curricula were developed by the Department of Physical Education, Health and Recreation: *Prosthetics and Orthotics* and *Physical Education and The Dance.*

In September 1961 the University Board of Trustees approved the establishment of the Department of Educational Theory and Application to incorporate a new approach to undergraduate professional education.

In several departments, among them the Departments of Educational Psychology, Educational Sociology and Anthropology, and Guidance and Personnel Administration, new emphases have been placed in courses and research projects on the possible corrosive effects on children and adults in a world of conflict and crisis. This has resulted in attempts to more closely integrate the social and behavioral sciences.

In home economics, grants have been made through the federal government and other agencies for studies of the special problems of the disadvantaged and for closer investigation of the relationship of nutrition to genetic factors. This brings the basic sciences into greater play than ever before in the work of this department.

In his latest annual report, the dean called attention to the major achievements of the School of Education during 1963–64:

1] The past year marked completion of plans by the Commission on Coordinated Liberal Studies for initiating in September 1964 All-University offerings in the liberal studies. Our administrative planning proceeded effectively in cooperation with the other divisions of the University.

2] Another important step toward All-University cooperation was the establishment of the Commission on Teacher Education. Recommended by us, this Commission will assure cooperation and coordination in teacher education in our University so that all students interested in teaching as a career should benefit regardless of the School in which they are matriculated.

3] Among curriculum developments that took place this past year, the following should be noted. The Department of English and Speech Education reported new graduate courses in the teaching of English as a second language as part of the International Students Program in Washington Square College. Three of the Departments of Educational Psychology teacher-training programs, mental retardation, hearing impairment, and orthopedic handicaps, were approved by the New York State Department of Education. Such approval makes it possible for teachers who wish to qualify in those areas of the physically exceptional child to receive grants from the State to cover the cost of tuition for all courses required for certification. State training grant arrangements were made for 40 students this past year. This year marks the 30th anniversary of the introduction of a modern course in Hebrew at New York University as the first of its kind in American higher education. Plans are being developed to commemorate this event.

4] The adoption of a revised undergraduate curriculum in the Department of Nurse Education. It is designed to provide education in nursing for college freshmen, transfer students, and registered nurse graduates of associate degree and hospital schools.

5] The Department of Art Education reported the addition of a high school painting workshop established for the artistically gifted high school youth. This course promises to recruit talented young people for art education programs at New York University.

6] One important step taken this year was toward reorganization of the School of Education into fewer administrative units. Fifteen faculty members comprising a Dean's Committee on Reorganization moved swiftly and favorably under the capable guidance of Associate Dean John C. Payne to a final meeting at which four reorganization patterns were submitted for consideration. These recommendations are now under review. We look to reorganization to help us speed our improvement of school-wide programs and services, and to produce a material reduction in overlapping and duplication of courses.

7] We are gratified to report that not only has the quality of our undergraduate students improved as admissions requirements have been raised, but the number of graduates has held firm. Graduate enrollment has increased, and we anticipate a continuation of this trend. Further, we are pleased to report that anticipated decreases in Fall 1964 freshman enrollments due to improved admissions' requirements will not occur to the degree that we had estimated.

8] Student personnel services constitute an important correlate to the teaching-learning process. We can report that Assistant Dean Florence N. Beaman and the counselling staff and some 60 faculty advisors, have had an active year. Students are becoming increasingly aware of the value of these services. Under the stimulus of Dean Beaman's office, students participated in student activities, student council, and other opportunities to broaden their collegiate experiences. Particularly important this year was a proposal to adjust advisement scheduling and assignment to assure that faculty-student relationships will contribute to student success. To help students adjust better to college life, a number of freshman counselors will work as a guidance team with Dean Beaman.

9] School-sponsored conferences including: The Junior High School Conference on Education of the Culturally Disadvantaged; Foreign Languages Conference; United Nations Symposium; Alumni Career Day for Juniors and Seniors; Vocational Education Spring Conference; Administration and Supervision Internship Conference; Implications of the Conant Report; Dual Progress Plan. The Graduate Students

Organization conducted an important three-day Education Fair.

10] The conference sponsored by the School of Education Advisory Council held at International Business Machines Corporation Laboratories on "The Implications of Technology for the School of Education." Another outstanding conference was "Integrating the Educational Progress Through the Curriculum," sponsored by our Department of Early Childhood and Elementary Education. Mention should also be made of the Puerto Rican Conference on "Educating New Yorkers of Puerto Rican Origin," which was held at Loeb Student Center for the fourth successive year.

On the eve of three quarters of a century of pioneering and progress, Dean Anderson's statement from the same report seems most appropriate:

The past year has been exciting and productive for the School of Education. Important steps have been taken toward our becoming *the* School of Education of the future. Our educational objectives and our mission have been revised and clarified. We have joined with other units of the university to develop plans for making New York University the outstanding private urban institution.

The School of Education has come a long way since a small group of pioneers embarked upon the first teacher-training program established as an integral part of a university. The pioneering spirit has been sustained through these seventy-five years by constant reappraisal and developmental changes looking toward improvement in service to the profession and the introduction of programs and experiences consonant with the recurring demands of an expanding culture. This ever broadening concept of professional education has witnessed the entry of faculty and administration into many types of activities and experiences beyond classroom teaching. They have answered the call to engage in private and public research projects and to work in many vineyards at home and abroad, wherever the challenge to assist in the improvement of the human condition has come.

The experiment with teacher training at the University level begun by the School of Pedagogy and the subsequent growth of the School of Education of New York University in these seventy-five years may be likened somewhat to the words of Stephen Vincent Benet: "You drop a stone in a pool and the circles spread. But on what far shore of the pool does the last circle break?" It would be interesting indeed to conjecture on what may be some far shore in the future. The moment permits but a brief speculation.

9 · A Look Ahead

The June, 1964 edition of the *New York University Alumni News* devotes its front page to the announcement of a Ford Foundation grant of $25,000,000 which, the headline states, "Reflects NYU's Leadership in Private Urban Education." The article submits that "few, if any, moments in New York University's one hundred and thirty-three years carried the dramatic intensity of the announcement" of the gift.

The terms of the grant will require the cooperation of alumni, non-alumni, foundations, and corporations to add another $75,000,000 within five years. President James McNaughton Hester, under whose leadership the donor expects this University to reach new levels of achievement, said, "This may well be the greatest day in the history of New York University. . . . This magnificent grant is the strongest possible encouragement to the full realization of the University's potential . . ."

As a member of the University family, the School of Education has a vital stake in contributing to the dynamic role of the University by increasing and extending its own.

In an article entitled "the New American Teacher," Dean Anderson takes the position that more well-qualified students are coming into teacher-education programs to-day—more intelligent, better informed, and more competent to start with. These individuals look to the college for stimulation through innovations, research findings, and new developments. "Every problem of society," Anderson asserts, "comes in the school door and on to the teacher's desk and into the teacher's classroom." [1] The modern teacher, the new teacher, must know how to deal with them.

In April, 1963, a statement of the mission of the School of Education was prepared by Dean Anderson, Associate Dean Griffiths and Associate Dean Payne. This statement makes clear that it is the aim of the School of Education to achieve three goals in the coming decade which should go far to provide the New American teacher with the fundamental tools essential for the effective execution of his task. These goals are:

1] to prepare superior teachers, administrators, and educational specialists for the schools, colleges, educational agencies, and professional organizations of the United States and other countries,

2] to pioneer in educational research and experimentation which creates new and useful knowledge for education generally and for teacher education in particular, and

3] to strengthen and improve education by providing professional services of the highest quality to schools and colleges and to other educational agencies at home and abroad.

[1] Walter A. Anderson, "A Look at the New American Teacher," *Mid-Hudson Channel.* Vol. 14, No. 2, Spring, 1964, pp. 7–11. Published by Mid-Hudson School Study Council, State University College, New Paltz, New York.

With the achievement of these goals, the report continues, the School will be characterized by excellence in all its preparation programs, by enlightened experimental programs and a new research emphasis, by significant educational services in the metropolitan New York Area, within the United States, and internationally.

The faculty and administration of the teacher-education unit accept the following rationale for a new mission for the division:

The School of Education as a professional school within a major university must take as its mission the creation and dissemination of knowledge through teaching, research, and service both at home and abroad. At the undergraduate level, the students of the School of Education will be taught by professors of the liberal studies from the entire University.

At the graduate level, students will be equipped with the knowledge and skill which will mark them as enlightened and creative professionals.

The School of Education has no desire to graduate professional educators dedicated to the maintenance of the status quo, but rather to prepare those who will create continously the 'new education'. . . . The School of Education plans to prepare professionals who will have commitment and purpose, who will have the political and social know-how to put the purpose into action, and the wit and wisdom to teach, research, and serve wisely and well.

The new program of the School is predicated on five assumptions concerning the role New York University should play in American education. These assumptions are:

1] The School of Education should remain a large institution.

2] The School of Education believes that teacher education is a university-wide function.

3] The School of Education should emphasize its graduate division, but at the same time develop an experimental undergraduate division.

4] The School of Education should be multi-purposed.

5] The School of Education should increasingly stress the creation of knowledge.

There are sound bases for confidence that the plans of the division can be successfully accomplished. Admissions procedures have been upgraded to insure a student body of high quality at both the undergraduate and graduate levels. This, it is hoped, will mean preparation of superior personnel for American education. The increase in private and public scholarships, fellowships, and grants makes it possible for more individuals to go on for advanced degrees and to enlarge the output of professional research, thus insuring continued improvement in theory and practice within diverse areas.

It has been accepted that the University's new purposes and goals, the new mission of the School of Education, and a new national climate for education are important incentives to change in organization and structure, and such change is contemplated.

The new building for the School of Education and the New York University School for Children now seem assured. These improvements will facilitate the on-going concept of service to the community and the profession to which the School is pledged.

The new emphasis on research will be continued by encouraging meaningful and needed experimental studies and by stimulating and enlarging faculty to take part in basic and applied research. More than $2,000,000 has been subscribed for research activity in each of the past two years.

The stature of this institution has been enhanced by the employment of Professor Jean Noble to assist Sargent Shriver, director of the nationwide poverty program now being launched by the federal government, and the selection of the School of Education by the United States Department of Labor as the New York State Training Center for the national Counselor Advisory University Summer Education(CAUSE) program. This program will involve the training of counselors for positions in centers to be established in state employment agencies affiliated with the United States employment services. Dr. Martin Hamburger, of the Department of Guidance and Personnel Administration, will serve as program supervisor at New York University.

The theme of the *Education Violet* (Yearbook) for 1964 is The Changing Face of New York University. Members of the administration—both central and School —in their greetings to the Class of 1964 each, in turn, refers to *change—change* in the social order, in the physical plant of the University, in the educational experiences provided at the University—and each cautions the graduate that he or she must be prepared to face and meet change. Change truly appears to be a watchword of this era of problems and crisis in which we still live. We have seen it in the world around us, and it is evident in this chronicle of a single educational institution. Change per se, however, need not be synonymous with progress. Therefore, the true educator must make the assessment of such change a permanent crusade, for as Buckingham, in discussing certain trends in education, has written: "Fundamentally, these changes have improved means but not ends. From them we have obtained convenience without contentment and change without stability. They have made war more terrible, peace more difficult, and the heart of Man more troubled." [2]

The problem of the twentieth century and probably of other centuries to come is how the constructive forces in modern society can best direct their efforts to influence and develop the deeper sources of the life of a people. Many forces must cooperate in such a task, but to the schools falls the greater share of the responsibility. In turn, schools cannot effectively discharge their function in this high endeavor unless their agents, the teachers, are individuals of high purpose and qualification. In the final analysis, then, it becomes the responsibility of institutions engaged in the preparation of men and women for service in all areas of education.

In the University's education unit at Washington Square the attitude of the administration and faculty toward this commitment to society is reflected in the words of Dean Anderson: "We look to the future with enthusiasm. We are confident that our mission is sound, and that we can implement it."

[2] B. R. Buckingham, "Permanent Educational Values in a World of Change," *Journal of Higher Education*, Vol. XXVII, No. 7, October, 1956, pp. 351–58.

10 · A Word About the Alumni

The School of Education stands more firmly entrenched on Washington Square than the famous hangman's tree in the northwest corner of the square. The "Tree of Knowledge " on the east side of the Square, while not sharing the function of the tree to the west, may be imagined to share its constructs. The tree which we may visualize as representing the institution has roots which are the deep, fundamental knowledges and tools of our accumulated heritage. The trunk, a connecting body between roots and further growth, is the faculty and administration through which this heritage is transmitted and enlarged. And its branches are the students and alumni, first absorbing, and then reaching out to spread this heritage and to create further growth of ideas and principles as the branches put out new and discard old leaves in the age-old life cycle.

The School of Education is a healthy tree, for its alumni are sturdy and productive branches.

The reorganized teacher-education unit at New York University had not gone through its first decade before an enthusiastic and active alumni association was under way. Faculty sponsorship, primarily through the tireless efforts of Dr. Charles E. Skinner, gave it impetus, and Dr. John J. Loftus, then superintendent of schools of New York City, was its first president.

The roster of officers of the School of Education Alumni Association is a veritable "Who's Who in Education." A list of those who have served as president of the association is given at the end of this section. A comparison of their class dates with the dates of office bespeaks the sustained interest and years of service among those who have held this office; nor does the expiration of that term of office imply termination of association. Dr. Lenore Vaughn-Eames, Dr. Herbert A. Tonne, and Dr. John J. Forrester—to name only three—are as active today as they have been in every year following graduation from the School. Under the stimulation and encouragement of these men and women, the membership of the association and its role have grown and have taken on increasing significance in relation to the affairs and the welfare of alma mater.

In the early years annual luncheons were held mainly to provide an opportunity for former classmates and faculty to renew old acquaintances and be brought up to date by Dean Withers on achievements and projections of the School.

Growing out of the sobering experiences of the 1930s and 1940s, it was concluded that such annual meetings should provide professional as well as social stimulation. Beginning in 1945 and continuing to the present, the annual spring conferences of the School of Education Alumni Association have revolved about a timely topic or theme. A partial list of these themes indicates keen sensitivity to the critical issues of the times:

1931 Truth and Illusion in Education
1935 A General Picture of Education at the Present Time
1938 Ten Years of the School of Education Alumni Association
1939 "Knowledge Comes but Wisdom Lingers" (use of a quotation from Tennyson)
1941 Fifty Years of American Education
1943 What Will Be the Part of the United States After the War?
1945 Education for International Understanding
1947 Education's Challenge: Reconciliation and Technological Developments
1950 Your School in One World
1952 The School of Education of the Future: Community Education for a World Society
1953 Alumni Participation and Integration of Teachers Education and Community Life
1954 Public Education: Whose Responsibility?
1956 Some Current Plans and Programs in the School of Education
1957 New York University and the Future of American Education (celebrated the 125th anniversary of NYU and the 100th anniversary of the NEA)
1959 Reassessing Values in American Education
1961 The Challenge to Education for the Next Decade
1963 Recent Developments in Education as they affect the School of Education
1964 Exploring Teacher Education—1964

The alumni group gives more than lip service to promoting the advancement of its chosen School. Through the establishment of special committees, studies have been undertaken by the Education alumni ranging all the way from an evaluation of the Department of Educational

Sociology back in 1940 to more recent studies of the master's program and the requirements and procedures governing doctors' degrees. On several occasions the deans have invited alumni participation in dealing with specific problems, and today members are working with the administration on plans for the new School of Education building. In addition, the School of Education Advisory Committee looks to such men as Dr. John Forrester, superintendent of schools at Uniondale, New York, and Dr. Walter Crewson, associate commissioner of education for New York State, for guidance and direction in mapping out the future, and to Dr. Walter Hartung '28E, ('57) Ed., who is now president of the New York University Alumni Federation.

Since the 1950s, alumni activities have included:

Career Day,
Faculty-Alumni reception,
Pre-Commencement Convocation,
Foreign-student orientation,
Establishment of the Ernest O. Melby award for distinguished service in the field of human relation,
Recognition of long and faithful service to the University by establishment of Fifteen, Twenty-five, and Thirty-five years service awards to faculty members,
Assistance in manning New York University headquarters at National Conventions,
Since 1960, service on Advisory Council to give advice and aid so that the School can better achieve its objectives.

From the days of the School of Pedagogy, which numbered among its alumni Julia Richman, Joseph Abelson, Jacob Theobald, Jacob Greenberg and Joseph Jablonower, alumni have continued to enter upon distinguished service. This is borne out by comparing cumulative data collected at the time of the institution's fiftieth year with data submitted by John Buckey, Director of New York University Placement Service, covering partial sample placements in the last five years. The figures indicate number of School of Education graduates in given positions:

Type of Position	Cumulative Number Employed at Bi-Centennial	Number Placed Since 1958
College President	1	5
College Vice-President	1	1
Dean	7	6
Other Administrative Officers	68	24
Professor	1843	63
College Teacher-Intern	—	30
Superintendent of Schools	60	40
Assistant Superintendent of Schools	8	22
Principal	237	116
Vice-Principal (or Asst.)	72	39
Supervisor—Coordinator	192	22
Business Staff—Ed. Institute	10	10

These figures suggest that the high caliber of graduates has been maintained since they continue to occupy significant posts throughout the country and abroad.

The business of school-alumni relationships is a two-way affair in the School of Education, and the list following represents seven points which are considered by the faculty and administration as important obligations if good relationships are to be maintained:

I. *Meetings with Alumni*
   1] The need to carry our meetings into small communities rather than merely having one big meeting

at NYU. Explore advantages of alumni meetings in the field.

2] Visits by members of the faculty to the schools of school administrators who are alumni.

3] Have many conferences at Washington Square in which alumni are invited to participate. Provide opportunities for our alumni to meet and become acquainted with the School of Education Staff.

II. *Keeping Alumni Informed of Developments in School of Education and NYU in General*

1] Keep alumni informed of on-going activities of the University. Involve as many alumni as possible in overall planning. Develop more activities to give present students a sense of belonging.

III. *Aid Alumni in their Professional Growth*

1] Help alumni to make progress in their profession through appointment service, appropriate course offerings, and development of new areas of education.

2] Our school should have more ways of serving its alumni.

3] Keep alumni informed of research findings at NYU, experiments in teaching, new emphases in education, available consultants, and field courses.

4] Follow-up studies of alumni to know their needs and interests. Solicitation of opinions of alumni concerning value of their studies in the School of Education.

IV. *Alumni Cooperation in Student Recruitment at NYU*

1] How can alumni aid us to obtain more and better students in both undergraduate and graduate divisions.

2] Arrange for visits to our School of Education of high school students who are interested in teaching as a career.

V. *Alumni Cooperation with NYU Placement Services*

1] We need more alumni activity in our placement services.

VI. *Keeping Track of our Alumni*

1] We need to develop a method to keep alumni addresses up to date.

VII. *Develop Membership in the Education Alumni Association of NYU*

    1] Identify seniors and graduate students with the Education Alumni Association while they are yet in college.

    2] Urge all faculty members to become members of the Education Alumni Association. A strong alumni association requires strong faculty participation and support.

        —Report from faculty Committee on Alumni and Public Relations based on suggestions from deans, department chairmen, and coordinators.

There may be some who have earned degrees and have gone their ways without strong convictions about almuni membership. For such persons it may be of interest at this point to reveal answers given by a charter member to the question "Why join the NYU School of Education Alumni Association." In her article entitled "Why Belong," she wrote:

Why belong to any association? Why belong to alumni associations? Specifically, why join, why belong to the New York University School of Education Alumni Associaton?

Because one cannot move among young people today without discovering their hunger for the ideal and the spiritual and their unrecognized revulsion against a materialistic outlook on life, let us consider first some of the higher and more altrustic reasons for joining the New York University School of Education Alumni.

1. Gratitude is an old-fashioned virtue, but its expression brings warmth to the one who receives it, and both warmth and spiritual growth to the one who feels it in his heart and tells it. Hence, I place it first among the reasons for joining an alumni association.

Second on my list is service. Sometimes we feel grateful and want to show it effectively, but we feel helpless and ignorant about how and what to do. The best and most immediate service we can give is to join the Alumni Association.

Concretely applied to the School of Education, this reason of service is really foremost. Also, the service is deserved and needed. The program and increased opportunities of NYU School of Education are among the most remarkable events in the history of the past ten years. Other institutions regard the results already attained with respect.

Third on my list is that much berated word, loyalty. Call me an antediluvian, if you wish, but let me retain my belief in loyalty, also my practice and preaching of loyalty.

Personally, I feel deeply these three motives of gratitude, service, and loyalty to the School of Education of New York University. Whatever weight my personal word, or personal example may carry is joyfully given with only the one regret that it cannot reach farther.

Neither space nor time permits an enlargement upon other reasons for joining our alumni organization . . . but I cannot omit brief mention of two of these. First, or rather fourth in my complete list is professional spirit, and fifth is the spirit of human progress.

A strongly welded alumni association in a school of education is a marvelous agent in developing a live, professional spirit.

The spirit of human progress is inextinguishable. The only question is whether you will have any share in that progress. Therefore, again, the Alumni Association of your School of Education—because education is the great instrument in human progress, and in so far as you aid in developing education, and in building unity, loyalty and professional spirit among educational workers, you have had a share in human progress.[1]

[1] "Why Belong," *Educational Service*, Vol. I, No. 3, April, 1929, pp. 3–5. Published by Alumni Association of the School of Education of New York University.

These reasons seem as pertinent today as they did in 1929. Perhaps, in the intensified atmosphere of change and need which colleges face today and will continue to face, each graduate of the School of Education of New York University will find his own personal and compelling reason for sharing in the progressive development of his alma mater.

Presidents

School of Education Alumni Association
1928–29—1964–65

1928–29—John J. Loftus, '23
1929–30— "   "   "
1930–31—Charles H. Cheney, '26
1931–32—James C. Bay, '27
1932–33— "   "   "
1933–34—Mary A. Kennedy, '26
1934–35— "   "   "
1935–36—Herbert Harper, '36
1936–37—Herman A. Ernst, '29
1937–38—Alice V. Crow, '27
1938–39—H. Claude Hardy, '39
1939–40—Clarence Dupee, '37
1940–41—Laura B. Harney, '39
1941–42—Herschel Libby, '32, '49
1942–43—Chris A. Rossey, '41
1943–44—Ira M. Kline, '27
1944–45—Alice M. Connor, '27, '32, '44
1945–46—Erie H. LeBarron, '46
1946–47—Lenore Vaughn-Eames, '24, '29, '38

1947–48—Philip A. Jakop, '39
1948–49—Charles Muschell, '38, '50
1949–50—John J. Forrester, '33
1950–51—Anna May Jones, '36
1951–52—Paul S. Lomax, '27
1952–53—Melvin Wagner, '32, '42
1953–54—Edw. J. Ambry, '45
1954–55—Irene F. Cypher, '40
1955–56—Edw. J. Ambry, '45
1956–57—Lawrence Mason, '40
1957–58—Frank Piazza, '39
1958–59—Bernard Schneider, '48
1959–60—Carol Cordes Smith,
1960–61—Joseph Grimes, '48
1961–62—David J. Brittain, '59
1962–63—Herbert A. Tonne, '27
1963–64—Paul Rossey, '53
1964–65—Marie A. Soscie, '45

Chairmen of Departments
School of Education
1921–65

Department	Name	Term of Service
Administration and Supervision	John W. Withers	1921–29
	A. B. Meredith	1929–41
	Pliny Powers	1941–44
	Emerson Langfitt (Acting)	1944–47
	Walter A. Anderson	1947–57
	Parmer L. Ewing	1957–64
	Richard C. Lonsdale	1964–
Adult Education	John Carr Duff	1948–58
Art Education	Robert A. Kissack	1926–46
	Robert Iglehart	1947–55
	Howard Conant	1955–
Business Education	Paul S. Lomax	1927–55
	Peter L. Agnew	1955–60
	Herbert A. Tonne	1960–
Center for Human Relations	H. Harry Giles	1949–56
	Dan W. Dodson	1956–
College Education	John O. Creager	1926–42
Communication Arts Group	Harvey W. Zorbaugh	1956–60
	Richard J. Goggin, Acting Executive Officer	1961–

Department	Name	Term of Service
Communications in Education	Charles A. Siepmann	1951–
Coordinated Teacher Training (Supervised Student Teaching)	Frithiof C. Borgeson Lyman B. Graybeal Glenn Thompson	1935–45 1946–49 1950–
Creative Education	Hughes Mearns	1923–45
Dramatic Art	Randolph Somerville Fred C. Blanchard John C. McCabe III	1934–55 1955–61 1961–
Early Childhood and Elementary Education	Margaret Noonan Dean Withers (Acting) Robert K. Speer Samuel McLaughlin Clara Platt Robert Fleming George Manolakes Alfred Ellison	1923–26 1926–29 1929–53 1953–55 1955–56 1956–60 1960–64 1964–
Educational Psychology	Charles E. Benson Brian E. Tomlinson John Rockwell Edward L. Kemp Charles E. Skinner Brian E. Tomlinson Edward L. Kemp (Acting)	1929–43 1945–56 1956–57 1957–58 1958–59 1959–62 1962–63 1963–
Educational Sociology and Anthropology	E. George Payne Harvey W. Zorbaugh Martin Bressler Dan W. Dodson	1923–45 1945–60 1960–63 1963–
English and Speech Education	Howard R. Driggs Thomas C. Pollack Walter Barnes (Acting) Thomas C. Pollock George R. Cerveny	1931–41 1941–43 1943–44 1944–47 1947–52

Department	Name	Term of Service
	Dorothy Mulgrave (Acting)	1953–56
	Harry G. Cayley	1956–59
	Elmer E. Baker, Jr. (Acting)	1959–60 1960–
Experimental Education and Educational Research	Paul R. Radosavljevich	1929–44
Foreign Languages and Literature (International Relations Education added as of 1960)	Rollin T. Tanner	1930–42
	Henri C. Olinger	1942–53
	Christian O. Arndt Foreign Languages and Director of Center of International Affairs	1953– 1960–
Guidance and Personnel Administration	Anna Y. Reed (Personnel Administration)	1927–39
	Robert Hoppock	1939–52
	Velma Hayden	1952–55
	William D. Wilkins	1955–64
	Milton Schwebel	1964–
Hebrew Culture and Education	Abraham I. Katsh	1953–
Higher Education	Alonzo F. Myers	1942–60
	Ellis White	1960–
History and Philosophy of Education	Herman H. Horne	1929–42
	Louise Antz (Acting)	1942–46
	George Axtelle	1946–53
	Louise Antz (Acting) Philosophy of Education	1953–57
	William W. Brickman (Acting) History of Education	1953–57
	George Axtelle	1957–59
	William Gruen (Acting)	1959–61 1961–64

Department	Name	Term of Service
	Henry J. Perkinson	1964–
Home Economics	Freda J. G. Winning	1928–37
	Dora Lewis	1937–45
	Anna K. Banks	1945–46
	Henrietta Fleck	1946–
Music Education	Hollis Dann	1925–36
	Ernest G. Hesser	1936–42
	Joseph R. Burns	1942–46
	Vincent Jones	1946–55
	Paul Van Bodegraven	1955–
Normal School, Teachers' College Education	Ambrose L. Suhrie	1929–40
Nurse Education	Vera Fry	1948–54
	Martha Rogers	1954–
Physical Education, Health and Recreation	Clark W. Hetherington	1925–29
	Jay B. Nash	1929–53
	Leonard A. Larson (Act.)	1953–55
		1955–59
	Morey Fields (Acting)	1959–60
		1960–62
	Raymond Weiss (Acting)	1962–63
		1963–
Religious Education	Samuel L. Hamilton	1931–50
	J. Campbell Wyckoff	1950–54
	Lee Belford	1954–
Safety Education	Herbert J. Stack	1953–61
	Walter Cutter	1961–
Science and Mathematics Education	Jacob A. Drushel, Mathematics	1929–38
	Charles J. Pieper, Science	1931–38
	Charles J. Pieper, Science and Mathematics	1938–49
	Charles J. Pieper, Science	1949–52

Department	Name	Term of Service
	John Kinsella, Mathematics	1949–57
	Darrell Barnard, Science	1953–57
	Darrell Barnard, Science and Mathematics	1957–
Secondary Education	P. W. L. Cox	1923–40
	Forrest E. Long (Acting)	1940–41
		1941–52
	Earl R. Gabler	1952–57
	William Van Till	1957–
Social Studies	Charles M. Gill	1927–40
	Daniel C. Knowlton	1940–42
	Samuel P. McCutchen (Acting)	1942–43
		1943–
Vocational Education	R. E. Pickett	1927–47
	William P. Sear, Jr.	1948–52
	Ray E. Haines and Roland H. Spaulding, Co-Chairmen	1952–55
	Robert L. Thompson	1955–58
	Raymond Van Tassel (Acting)	1958–59
		1959–

A view of Washington Square of the future as conceived by architect Philip Johnson. A special feature of the design concept is a campus arcade, with an arched roof of glass and steel across Washington Place between the Main and Education buildings.

Walter A. Anderson, Dean 1960–1964

"We look to the future with enthusiasm. We are confident that our mission is sound, and that we can implement it."